SDL Trados Studio – A Practical Guide

Learn how to translate more efficiently with SDL Trados Studio 2014

Andy Walker

BIRMINGHAM - MUMBAI

SDL Trados Studio – A Practical Guide

First published: February 2014

Production Reference: 1140214

Published by Packt Publishing Ltd.
Livery Place
35 Livery Street
Birmingham B3 2PB, UK.

ISBN 978-1-84969-963-1

www.packtpub.com

Cover Image by Duraid Fatouhi (duraidfatouhi@yahoo.com)

Credits

Author
Andy Walker

Reviewers
Jerzy Czopik
Alison Field
Daniela Ford

Acquisition Editors
Nikhil Karkal
Rubal Kaur
Mary Jasmine Nadar

Commissioning Editor
Poonam Jain

Technical Editors
Shubhangi Dhamgaye
Pratik More

Copy Editors
Janbal Dharmaraj
Alfida Paiva

Project Coordinator
Aboli Ambardekar

Proofreader
Joanna McMahon

Indexer
Mehreen Deshmukh

Production Coordinator
Manu Joseph

Cover Work
Manu Joseph

Foreword

Life as a professional translator today is a completely different kettle of fish to what it was only 25 years ago. Translators are no longer "just" linguists—many have to embrace translation technology in order to remain competitive or to even simply get that in-house or freelance translation job.

One of the major developments in translation technology has been Translation Memory Tools—software programs that became commercially available in the mid-1990s and started out as mere databases, which a translator could "fill" with original texts and their corresponding translations, and which would then serve as the translator's memory. If the translator translated another text that contained identical or even similar sentences, the translation memory would search automatically (in the background) whether a translation already existed, and if so, would insert this translation automatically into the new file for translation. It all seemed magical at the time, although it obviously wasn't!

Back in the day, Translation Memory software was small, shipped on 3.5-inch floppy disks, and the user guide consisted of some 30 pages, which a fairly computer-literate translator could peruse and then proceed to use the software straight away. Times have changed since then; there are now a lot of different Translation Memory tools from a number of vendors on the market. The software tends to be available for download only, and most tools no longer come with a printed user guide but a massive online help consisting of thousands of pages. The software itself has become a full-blown tool in many cases, with features such as terminology management, project management, and so forth added on.

Many Translation Memory tool vendors now offer online and face-to-face training sessions in order to assist users to learn how to use the tool. Similarly, many universities all over the world have recognized that their translation students need to know what a Translation Memory tool is and how to use it, and have therefore included translation memory in their curricula.

This book has a really practical focus and fills a big gap in the market. I can see the book being used by both fledgling and experienced translators to learn how to use SDL Trados Studio at their own pace. I can also see the book on the virtual and real bookshelves of university libraries and as a companion/reader on every university course that teaches SDL Trados Studio.

London, February 2014

Daniela Ford

Dipl.-Fachübersetzerin, MITI, Managing Director of Softrans Ltd,
Lecturer in Translation Technology at UCL and Imperial College London

About the Author

Andy Walker has worked for many years as a translator and is an experienced trainer and teacher of translation technology. He combines his work as a freelance translator (working from Japanese, French, and German into English) and Japanese-English interpreter with the post of a Senior Lecturer in Translation Technology at the University of Roehampton in London. As well as being a Member of the Institute of Translation and Interpreting (MITI), he is an Approved Trainer for SDL Trados Studio and currently one of SDL's Lecturer Champions.

I would like to thank my family, my colleagues at the University of Roehampton, and the staff of SDL for their support with the writing of this book. In particular, I would like to acknowledge the role of the technical reviewers Alison Field, Jerzy Czopik, and Daniela Ford. Their numerous insights, corrections, and suggestions have resulted in great many improvements to the content of the book.

About the Reviewers

Jerzy Czopik, born in Cracow, studied Mechanical Engineering at the Cracow Technical University. He finished his studies after relocating to Germany in 1986 at the University Dortmund. Since 1990, he has been a full-time translator and interpreter for German and Polish. He is a user of many CAT tools and trainer for SDL Trados products. He is an LICS auditor for the translation standard EN 15038.

He is the author of the manual *SDL Trados Studio 2009 dla (nie)wtajemniczonych*, published by *Biuro Marketingowe Adebik, 2011*, ISBN 8362134097.

Alison Field is a freelance technical translator, proofreader/reviewer, and trainer. She has worked in linguistics for some considerable time, covering virtually all aspects of the translation chain at some point in her career, seasoned with teaching French for enjoyment.

For many years, Alison worked for Balthasar Ltd, a small translation agency based in Herefordshire. This is a company that has built its success, firstly on the strength of a gifted, committed team, and secondly, by never compromising on its watchword: quality.

Through this experience and her own ongoing professional development, Alison became increasingly conversant, first with Trados, then SDL Studio, and of course MultiTerm. She progressed to becoming an invaluable member of the SDL beta testing team, which she finds highly rewarding.

Alison loves nothing better than "playing" with languages, especially using computer software to do so. She happily spends hours troubleshooting others' issues with CAT software, displaying all the tenacity of a Yorkshire terrier with a bone. When presented with an apparently insoluble problem, Alison's usual response is "hmm, that's interesting...", following which she might not surface again for a few hours until she has got right to the root of the problem, and probably solved several others along the way!

I would like to thank Andy for the honor of performing a technical review of his book, which I have thoroughly enjoyed.

Daniela Ford has an MSc in Technical Translation from the University of Hildesheim, Germany. She started her professional career in London where she worked for 5 years as an in-house translator (French/English into German) before going freelance in 1999 and then forming her own limited company. Her main subject areas are technical and software localization, and she works for many international blue-chip companies.

She has been teaching MSc Translation part-time at Imperial College London since 2001 (when the course was launched) and is continuing to teach it since the course was transferred to University College London, in 2013. She has also been involved in teaching a module on translation memory and machine translation at the University of Westminster in London, and is currently still teaching Translation Technologies at the University of Westminster as a visiting lecturer, as well as several other universities in and outside of London, including Doha (Qatar). She was involved in a three-year EU-funded project on creating e-learning courses for translators, and is the author and moderator of the e-learning course on Software Localization at Imperial College London, which is currently running for the 16th time and attracts participants from all over the world.

Daniela Ford is an SDL-certified trainer for SDL Trados technologies and has also given several talks at international conferences including Aslib Translating and The Computer (London) and the ITI (Institute of Translation & Interpreting) Conference in the UK. She is also a committee member of the London Regional Group of the ITI.

A keen reader and language enthusiast, she has learned around 10 languages so far in her life, and has a passion for everything related to language technologies including software development and localization.

Daniela Ford is married and lives and works in London.

www.PacktPub.com

Support files, eBooks, discount offers and more

You might want to visit www.PacktPub.com for support files and downloads related to your book.

Did you know that Packt offers eBook versions of every book published, with PDF and ePub files available? You can upgrade to the eBook version at www.PacktPub.com and as a print book customer, you are entitled to a discount on the eBook copy. Get in touch with us at service@packtpub.com for more details.

At www.PacktPub.com, you can also read a collection of free technical articles, sign up for a range of free newsletters and receive exclusive discounts and offers on Packt books and eBooks.

http://PacktLib.PacktPub.com

Do you need instant solutions to your IT questions? PacktLib is Packt's online digital book library. Here, you can access, read and search across Packt's entire library of books.

Why Subscribe?
- Fully searchable across every book published by Packt
- Copy and paste, print and bookmark content
- On demand and accessible via web browser

Free Access for Packt account holders

If you have an account with Packt at www.PacktPub.com, you can use this to access PacktLib today and view nine entirely free books. Simply use your login credentials for immediate access.

Shortcuts

Ctrl + Alt + Enter = Confirm + Next

Ctrl + Enter = Confirm + Next Unconfirmed

~~~~Concordance Search = F3

Alt + Shift + Insert = Copy $\boxed{All}$ Source to Target

Ctrl + Ins/Alt + Ins = Copy Source to Target

Ctrl + Alt + S = Merge Segments

Ctrl + ↑/↓ = move ↑/↓

Ctrl + M = next

Ctrl + Shift + M = previous

Source concordance search = Ctrl + F3

Alt + Shift + T = split segment

Target concordance search = Ctrl + Shift + F3

Ctrl + Shift + L = insert term
Ctrl + comma = insert Variable

Table of Contents

Preface

SDL Trados Studio – A Practical Guide is intended to be a practical guide to the use of **SDL Trados Studio 2014** which is both accessible to the novice and detailed enough to help more experienced users develop their knowledge further. Our intention has been to write in plain English, avoiding the use of unnecessary jargon, and to present information and instructions in self-contained sections corresponding to the tasks that users will likely need to perform in practice. For several chapters, we have created downloadable sample files so that readers can work along with the instructions, but the material in this book is equally intended as a source of reference for readers to use in their learning. The key tasks are organized into eight chapters, with topics for further exploration in two appendices. SDL Trados Studio 2014 is a tool that is rich in features, and much of the information presented in one chapter will of course apply equally in situations described in others. We hope that you will enjoy using this book.

What this book covers

Chapter 1, Getting Started with SDL Trados Studio, shows how to install and run SDL Trados Studio 2014 for the first time, navigate your way around the SDL Trados Studio 2014 interface, and customize it to your own way of working.

Chapter 2, Creating and Using Translation Memories, explains how to create a translation memory and select translation memories to use when you open a document for translation.

Chapter 3, Translating a File, shows how to translate a file in SDL Trados Studio, from opening a document to generating the translated version, including lots of practical tips and tricks for getting the best out of SDL Trados Studio while you translate. This chapter has a downloadable sample file to work along with.

Chapter 4, Formatting and Tags, explains how to work with visual formatting and tags to ensure that the formatting and functionality of your translated document is the same as that of the original. This chapter has a downloadable sample file to work along with.

Chapter 5, Word Counts and Billing Information, demonstrates how to produce a report showing the word count broken down into various types of match and use this information for quoting and billing. This chapter has a downloadable sample file to work along with.

Chapter 6, Editing and Quality Assurance, shows how to make the best of SDL Trados Studio during the review process using features designed specifically to help you edit and check your work, such as Review mode, the Display Filter, Track Changes, Comments, and the QA Checker. This chapter has a downloadable sample file to work along with.

Chapter 7, Working with Projects, explains how to use a project both to preserve and re-use your translation settings and to translate a set of files as a part of the same job. This chapter also shows how to use project packages to share the material in a project with another person.

Chapter 8, Managing Terminology, shows how to create a termbase for storing terminology and other chunks of text, which can then be used to recognize and display term matches automatically during translation.

Appendix A, Working with Files from Earlier Versions of Trados, indicates how to upgrade SDL Trados 2007 translation memories and use bilingual Translator's Workbench and TagEditor files in SDL Trados Studio.

Appendix B, Managing Translation Memories, explains how to import and export translation memory data in SDL Trados Studio translation memories and selectively modify or delete their content. This chapter also explains how to use the alignment feature to recycle content from existing pairs of documents (source and translation) that were translated without using a translation memory tool by aligning them for use in an SDL Trados Studio translation memory.

What you need for this book

To follow the guidance and instructions in this book, you will need a functioning copy of SDL Trados Studio 2014 and SDL MultiTerm 2014.

Version of SDL Trados Studio used in this book

In this book, we work with SDL Trados Studio 2014 - 11.0.3636.0, the latest version of the software at the time of writing. We refer to the Professional and Freelance versions of SDL Trados Studio and indicate the relevant differences between them at the appropriate points in the book. For information on the available versions of SDL Trados Studio and the differences between them, please visit the SDL website at `http://www.sdl.com/products/sdl-trados-studio/index-tab4.html#10-1808`.

System requirements for SDL Trados Studio

"As a minimum requirement, we recommend a recent Microsoft Windows-based computer (including Intel-based Apple Mac computers running Windows as an operating system) with 2 GB RAM and a screen resolution of 1280x1024. For optimum performance on 64-bit operating systems, we recommend 4 GB RAM or more and a higher screen resolution."

SDL, `http://www.sdl.com/products/sdl-trados-studio/faqs.html#tag13` (February 2014)

Who this book is for

This book is designed both for new users and those who already have some knowledge of SDL Trados Studio. Its aim is to acquaint you with the key features of the program quickly and to help you enhance your knowledge through more in-depth exploration. No previous experience of translation memory programs is required, although it is assumed that readers will be comfortable working with standard MS Windows applications.

Conventions

In this book, you will find a number of styles of text that distinguish between different kinds of information. Here are some examples of these styles, and an explanation of their meaning.

Code words in text, database table names, folder names, filenames, file extensions, pathnames, dummy URLs, user input, and Twitter handles are shown as follows: "In the project folder, select the blue project file (`sdlproj`)".

New terms and **important words** are shown in bold. Words that you see on the screen, in menus or dialog boxes for example, appear in the text like this: "In the **Product Activation** dialog box, click the **Activate** button".

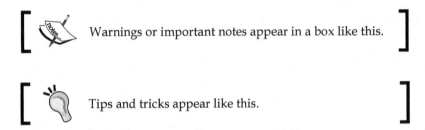

Warnings or important notes appear in a box like this.

Tips and tricks appear like this.

Reader feedback

Feedback from our readers is always welcome. Let us know what you think about this book—what you liked or may have disliked. Reader feedback is important for us to develop titles that you really get the most out of.

To send us general feedback, simply send an e-mail to feedback@packtpub.com, and mention the book title via the subject of your message.

If there is a topic that you have expertise in and you are interested in either writing or contributing to a book, see our author guide on www.packtpub.com/authors.

Customer support

Now that you are the proud owner of a Packt book, we have a number of things to help you to get the most from your purchase.

Downloading the sample files

The sample files for use with Chapters 3, 4, 5, and 6 can be downloaded from http://www.packtpub.com. If you purchased this book elsewhere, you can visit http://www.packtpub.com/support and register to have the files e-mailed directly to you.

Errata

Although we have taken every care to ensure the accuracy of our content, mistakes do happen. If you find a mistake in one of our books — maybe a mistake in the text or the code — we would be grateful if you would report this to us. By doing so, you can save other readers from frustration and help us improve subsequent versions of this book. If you find any errata, please report them by visiting `http://www.packtpub.com/submit-errata`, selecting your book, clicking on the **errata submission form** link, and entering the details of your errata. Once your errata are verified, your submission will be accepted and the errata will be uploaded on our website, or added to any list of existing errata, under the Errata section of that title. Any existing errata can be viewed by selecting your title from `http://www.packtpub.com/support`.

Piracy

Piracy of copyright material on the Internet is an ongoing problem across all media. At Packt, we take the protection of our copyright and licenses very seriously. If you come across any illegal copies of our works, in any form, on the Internet, please provide us with the location address or website name immediately so that we can pursue a remedy.

Please contact us at `copyright@packtpub.com` with a link to the suspected pirated material.

We appreciate your help in protecting our authors, and our ability to bring you valuable content.

Questions

You can contact us at `questions@packtpub.com` if you are having a problem with any aspect of the book, and we will do our best to address it.

1
Getting Started with SDL Trados Studio

In this chapter, we take you through the process of installing **SDL Trados Studio** and running it for the first time. You will then learn about the SDL Trados Studio interface: what the different panes, toolbars, and ribbon menus and tabs are for, and how to customize the interface to your own way of working. We also look at the help resources that SDL Trados Studio provides to support you as you work. The main sections in this chapter are as follows:

- Installing SDL Trados Studio
- Running SDL Trados Studio for the first time
- Navigating the interface
- Customizing the interface
- Getting help

Installing SDL Trados Studio

If you already have a previous version of SDL Trados or SDLX installed, there is no need to uninstall it before you install SDL Trados Studio 2014. To install Studio 2009 or 2011 on the same machine as Studio 2014, install Studio 2009 or 2011 first. For information on installing the 30-day trial version, visit `http://tinyurl.com/trados-studio-trial`.

To install SDL Trados Studio, click on the installation packages that you have downloaded and follow the instructions. Install SDL Trados Studio 2014 first, and then MultiTerm 2014. Note that SDL MultiTerm 2014 is not available in a trial mode.

You can install the **Freelance** version on more than one machine, but only one license can be active at a time. To use the Freelance version on another machine, first deactivate the current license by choosing **Help | Product Activation**, then run SDL Trados Studio on the other machine and activate the license as described in this chapter. Alternatively, you can purchase the **Freelance Plus** version, which allows you to activate licenses on two machines at the same time.

For full details on the installation procedure, download SDL's installation guide from `http://tinyurl.com/sdl-install-manual`.

Selecting languages when installing the Freelance version

In the Freelance version of SDL Trados Studio, the number of languages that you can work with is restricted to five, which you must choose during installation. Sublanguages such as French (France) and French (Canada) are counted as one language.

You cannot change the language selection after installation. To change the languages, you must deactivate, uninstall, and then reinstall SDL Trados Studio.

In the **Professional** version, there is no limit on the number of languages you can use, so it is not necessary to select languages during installation.

Running SDL Trados Studio for the first time

To run SDL Trados Studio for the first time after you install it, follow these steps:

1. To launch SDL Trados Studio on Windows 7, choose **Start | All Programs | SDL | SDL Trados Studio 2014** and click **SDL Trados Studio 2014**. Alternatively, click the SDL Trados Studio 2014 icon on your Windows desktop. On Windows 8, click the SDL Trados Studio 2014 icon on the desktop or the Metro screen, shown in the following screenshot:

2. The first time you run SDL Trados Studio, you must activate the product using the activation code that you received from SDL. In the **Product Activation** dialog box, click the **Activate** button (you will need an Internet connection to do this).

3. Copy and paste (or type) the activation code into the **Activation code** field, and then click the **Activate** button again, as shown in the following screenshot. The button highlighted on the right can be used to paste in the activation code from the clipboard. To continue in the 30-day trial mode, click the **Continue** button (this option may not be available if you have Studio 2014 and 2011 installed on the same machine. In this case, you may be able to obtain an activation code for the trial version. See `http://tinyurl.com/trados-trial`).

If this method of activation does not apply to you, click the **Alternative activation options** link. This enables you to activate the product offline, or use a license server. For information on activation issues, visit the **SDL Knowledge Base** at `http://kb.sdl.com/`.

4. Once you have activated the product, the setup wizard will be launched. The first screen is the **Welcome** screen, where you simply click **Next**.

5. On the **Current User Details** screen, type your name and e-mail address in the corresponding fields (this information is mandatory), and click **Next**.

6. On the **User Profile** screen, leave the user profile as **Default**, and click **Next**.

The other options, **SDLX** and **SDL Trados**, reflect some of the shortcuts and default settings in older versions of SDL Trados and SDLX, and may result in a behavior different from that described in this book in certain situations.

7. If you have installed the Professional version, go straight to step 8. If you have installed the Freelance version, the **Language Selection** screen will now appear, and you will be asked to choose five languages, as shown in the following screenshot. Choose a language from the list and click **Add**. When you have added five languages, click **Next**.

8. On the **Samples** screen, click **Finish** to complete the setup.

You will only have to follow the previously described setup process when running the product for the first time. However, in some shared public environments, where user-specific settings are deleted whenever a user logs off, for example, some university networks, you may have to run steps 3 to 6 to set up SDL Trados Studio each time you open it. The setup wizard may also run when a cumulative update installs, but this is not a cause for concern.

9. Finally, when SDL Trados Studio opens, you are prompted to sign up for the automated translation service, **BeGlobal**. Follow the wizard to sign up, or click **Cancel** to ignore (you can sign up later from within SDL Trados Studio).

Note that BeGlobal does not support all language pairs.

Navigating the interface

When SDL Trados Studio opens, you will see the **Welcome** screen, shown in the following screenshot:

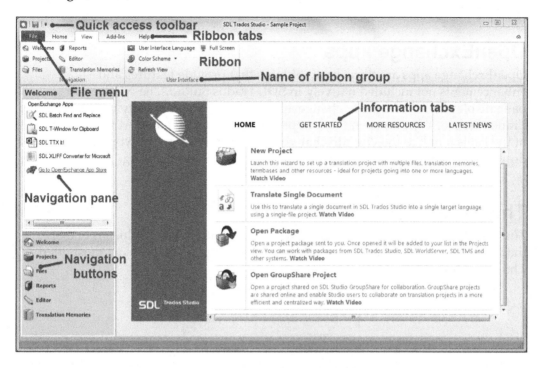

At the center of the **Welcome** screen, you will find common functions such as **Translate Single Document** (to select and open an individual file to translate in SDL Trados Studio), and **New Project** (to run the wizard to create a new project for translating one or more files based on certain predefined settings).

 In SDL Trados Studio, many of the most common commands are available in more than one place. The **Translate Single Document** function, for example, appears in the middle of the **Welcome** screen, in the **File** menu under **Open**, and can also be accessed by pressing the default shortcut *Ctrl + Shift + O*.

The Navigation pane

The Navigation pane on the left in the previous screenshot gives easy access to **OpenExchange** apps and to the navigation buttons crucial for navigating the interface.

OpenExchange apps

OpenExchange apps are third-party plugins that provide features and enhancements not included natively in SDL Trados Studio. The Navigation pane displays a list of OpenExchange apps installed automatically with SDL Trados Studio. You can open these apps directly from the pane. At the bottom of the list is a link to the **OpenExchange App Store**, from where you can download other apps. Many are free and well worth investigating.

The navigation buttons

The Navigation pane also contains the navigation button panel, which is one of the elements of the SDL Trados Studio interface that you will be using most often. The navigation button panel looks like this:

The buttons each give access to a different **view** in SDL Trados Studio. Each view contains features for performing a different set of tasks. For example, the **Editor** view is where you translate and edit your documents.

The application ribbon

SDL Trados Studio 2014 has a ribbon menu similar to that in recent versions of Microsoft Office.

The File menu

The **File** menu at the left-hand side of the ribbon is present in all views and contains the same commands in each view. It gives access to commonly used functions such as opening, closing, and reopening files; accessing recent documents; creating new files (such as documents for translation and translation memories); and saving and printing; as well as the **Options** menu for configuring various settings. The following screenshot shows part of the **File** menu with the **Open** command on the left-hand side:

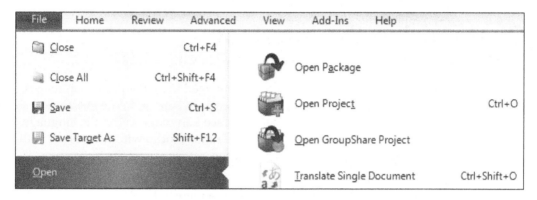

Ribbon tabs and groups

Each view contains different ribbon commands depending on the tasks performed in it. Each ribbon contains **Home**, **View**, **Add-Ins**, and **Help** tabs. The commands in each tab are divided into groups based on their functionalities. For example, the **Home** tab of the **Translation Memories** view, part of which is shown in the following screenshot, contains (among others) **Configuration**, **Tasks**, and **Tools** groups:

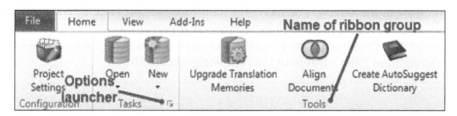

The **Home** tab generally contains essential commands for that view. The **View** tab generally contains commands for displaying and searching information. The **Add-Ins** tab is reserved for third-party add-ins (likely to be more fully realized in subsequent versions). For information on the **Help** tab, see the *Getting help* section later in this chapter.

To display a tool tip describing what each icon is for and showing its keyboard shortcut, hover over it with your mouse pointer. Press *Alt* in any window to display the hotkeys for accessing menu commands with a single button press.

Many of the command groups on the ribbon have an **Options launcher** icon at the bottom right, as highlighted in the preceding screenshot. Press this button to display further configuration options specific to this command group.

Customizing the interface

The SDL Trados Studio interface can be customized in various ways:

- **Language interface**: This interface can be changed to one of the six languages: English, French, German, Spanish, Japanese, and Chinese. In the **Welcome** view, from the **View** tab choose **User Interface Language**, select the language you want from the list, and click **OK**. SDL Trados Studio will then restart with the interface in the language you have chosen.

- **Minimize the ribbon**: At the top right of the interface, press the **Minimize the Ribbon** button, shown in the following screenshot:

  You can still access the ribbon commands by clicking the name of each view. To expand the ribbon, press the button again.

- **Fullscreen mode**: To go into the fullscreen mode, press *F11*. This minimizes the Navigation pane and ribbon, and increases the visible space in the middle of the screen. The navigation buttons remain visible when the pane is minimized. To exit the fullscreen mode, press *F11* again. You can also minimize the Navigation pane by clicking the button at the top right of the Navigation pane, shown in the following screenshot:

- **Reduced screen display space**: If you are working with a small screen on which the interface is squashed up, SDL Trados Studio will compensate for the lack of space by displaying the command icons without the corresponding text, or showing only the name of the command group. In the following screenshot from the **Editor** view, the hidden commands in the **Segment Actions** group are displayed by clicking the small arrow after the name of the group:

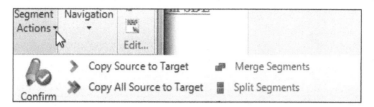

Getting help

To search the online help files, from the **Help** tab shown in the following screenshot, choose **Help Topics**, or press *F1* from anywhere in SDL Trados Studio:

The **Help** ribbon also gives access to **Tutorials** (instruction videos on SDL's YouTube site) and **SDL Knowledge Base** (a repository of answers to technical queries), and several other resources such as **SDL My Account** and **Product Activation**.

In the **Welcome** view, the information tabs in the middle of the screen also provide quick access to various helpful resources as follows:

- **GET STARTED**: This tab has a number of quick start guides and how-to videos

- **MORE RESOURCES**: This tab gives access to release notes, the migration guide, and so on

- **LATEST NEWS**: This tab provides information from SDL on the latest bug fixes, updates, and so on

You can also look for help and ideas in independent resources such as ProZ.com (the **SDL Trados support** forum) at `http://tinyurl.com/proz-trados`. The blog by SDL's *Paul Filkin* includes lots of useful articles on SDL Trados Studio and related topics (see `http://multifarious.filkin.com/`).

Summary

After working through this chapter, you should have SDL Trados Studio up and running on your machine and be able to find your way around the interface. In the next chapter, you will learn how to create a translation memory.

2

Creating and Using Translation Memories

A **translation memory (TM)** is a database used to store translations as you translate in a program such as SDL Trados Studio. If the document that you are translating contains sentences or other discrete units of text (known as segments) that are the same as, or similar to those in the TM, SDL Trados Studio will signal that a match has been found, and offer you the opportunity to recycle and (if necessary) edit the content, thereby making the process of translating quicker and more efficient. This chapter shows you how to create a TM and select TMs to use when you open a document for translation. We start by discussing how to organize your document folders for maximum efficiency.

Creating a folder structure

When you work with SDL Trados Studio to translate single documents as described in the following chapters, it is well worth taking the time to make an organized folder structure to store your files. For one thing, you will be creating more files than when you translate using only a program such as MS Word. Also, SDL Trados Studio will create some files automatically in the background. It is therefore essential that you know at all times where you are storing the files that you create, and where to find them when you need them.

Here, as an example, we have created a parent folder that will eventually contain all of the files used for this particular translation task. In the parent folder, we have created three subfolders to store our source files, target files, and TMs, as you can see in the following screenshot:

Of course, there are plenty of other ways to organize your material. The essential point is that you have an organized system that works for you. If you are working with a project rather than the **Translate Single Document** method referred to in this chapter, the folder structure is created automatically when you create the project. We will cover how to use SDL Trados Studio's project creation wizard later on in *Chapter 7, Working with Projects*.

Creating a translation memory

In this section, we take you through the basic steps for creating a TM, which you will use to store your translations and produce matches as you translate (we will go through this process in *Chapter 3, Translating a File*). In this section, we emphasize the importance of giving your TM an easily recognizable name and saving it in an organized folder structure so that you can safely find and recognize it at a later date. To create a new TM, take the following steps:

1. From the **File** menu, choose **New | New Translation Memory** (or press *Alt + Shift + N*) to launch the **New Translation Memory** wizard. When the **New Translation Memory** wizard launches, you will see the following screen:

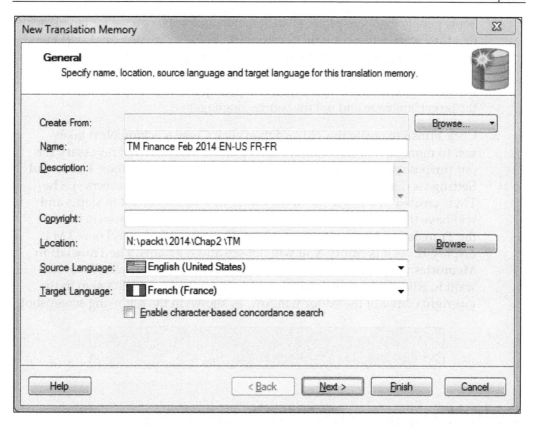

2. In the **Name** field, type a suitable name for your TM. If you use SDL Trados Studio frequently, you may, over time, create many TMs and will need to be able to tell them apart. Here, as an example, we indicate the subject, date, and language pair to help identify the TM more easily at a later point in time (whether from within SDL Trados Studio or from a list of files in Windows Explorer).

3. In the **Location** field, click **Browse** to go to the folder you created to store the TM. Once you select the folder, you will see the file path in the **Location** field.

4. Select the source and target languages.

    SDL Trados Studio differentiates between sublanguages such as French (France) and French (Canada). This means that if one TM has the source (or target) language as French (France) and another, French (Canada), they cannot be used together when translating a document in SDL Trados Studio.

Some people therefore prefer to stick to the same sublanguage for languages that they work with regularly (for example, always choosing English (United States) or Spanish (Spain)). If you use this approach for the target language, though, bear in mind that the spellchecker may pick upon differences between the sublanguages and display them as spelling errors (the spellchecker checks the target language and not the source language).

5. Click **Finish** to create the TM and then click **Close** (clicking **Next** takes you to more advanced configuration options, which are not necessary for our purpose of creating a basic TM. Of these advanced options, **Fields and Settings** is discussed in *Appendix B, Managing Translation Memories*). The TM is created as a single file in the folder that you specified in step 3 and will have the file extension .sdltm. SDL Trados Studio now switches to the **Translation Memories** view, where the (currently empty) new TM is displayed. As it is empty, you will not see any segments. The **Translation Memories** view is intended for editing work on the TM itself. We do not want to edit it now, so we will close it by pressing the small **X** sign in the top-right corner of the editor window, as shown in the following screenshot:

Selecting a translation memory

To use a TM during translation, you must first select it in SDL Trados Studio. To select a TM to work with when you open an individual document for translation in SDL Trados Studio, follow these steps:

1. From the **File** menu, choose **Open | Translate Single Document** or press *Ctrl + Shift + O*. Browse to the document that you want to open for translation, select it, and click **Open**.

2. In the **Open Document** dialog box, select the source and target languages (and sublanguages) to match those of your TM.

> To avoid having to reselect your language pair each time, you can change the default language pair under **File | Options | Editor | Languages**.

3. Choose **Add | File-based Translation Memory**, browse to select your TM, and click **Open**. The completed **Open Document** dialog box is shown in the following screenshot:

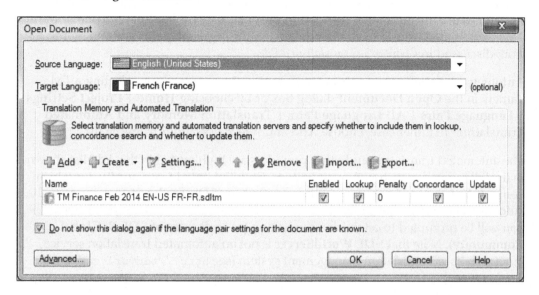

You may wish to uncheck the **Do not show this dialog again** checkbox to ensure that the **Open Document** dialog box will still appear when you next open a bilingual file whose language pair can be detected automatically, so that you can check or modify the TM selection before you open the document for translation.

 You can also create new TMs from the **Open Document** dialog box shown in the preceding screenshot. Click **Create** and follow the steps for creating a TM described previously.

4. Click **OK** to open the document for translation using this TM.

Using automated translation providers

You can use a number of automated translation providers to give you a rough translation in segments where there is no match from a TM. Translators therefore sometimes use an automated translation provider in combination with one or more TMs. Automated translations are indicated in the segment status column by the **AT** icon, discussed in *Chapter 3, Translating a File.*

Automated translation services are activated in the same way as selecting a TM, namely in the **Open Document** dialog box or by choosing **Home | Project Settings | Language Pairs | All Language Pairs | Translation Memory and Automated Translation**. In either case, choose **Add** and select a provider from the list.

The automated translation and other providers are highlighted in the **Add** list shown in the following screenshot. As you will see, **SDL BeGlobal Community**, for which you may be prompted to sign up when you first run SDL Trados Studio, is one such automated translation provider. Once you have selected one of these providers, you will be prompted to establish a connection (as in the case of **SDL BeGlobal Community**). Note that **SDL WorldServer** is not an automated translation service but a web-based translation management system (see `http://tinyurl.com/sdl-worldserver`).

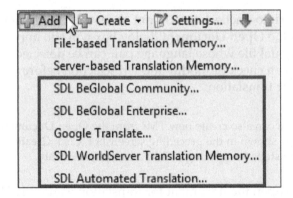

 At the time of writing, Google Translate requires you to set up an API key, the use of which may be chargeable. Users would also be well advised to check whether using an automated translation provider could put them in breach of any confidentiality agreements with their clients.

Working with more than one translation memory

SDL Trados Studio allows you to translate using several TMs at once. This is useful in the following situations:

- When you have more than one TM containing any material that you think might provide matches.

- When you want to use one TM to store new translations as you work (and produce matches based on that content while you translate), and another one purely for reference (that is to say, offering possible matches but not storing any new translations, and so remaining unchanged during the translation process).

Adding a further translation memory

To add a further TM during the process of opening a single document for translation, click **Add** and follow the steps described in the preceding section, *Selecting a translation memory*.

When you add a second TM, its **Update** box on the right will be *unchecked* by default, as shown in the following screenshot:

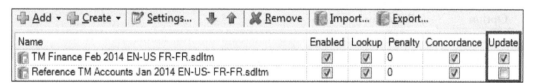

The **Update** setting defines whether or not your translations will be stored in the TM as you translate. When you add another TM, the **Update** box for that TM is unchecked. If you want the second TM also to store new translations as you translate, check the **Update** box for that TM.

 Normally, at least one of the TMs is set to update; otherwise, none of your translations will be stored in a TM as you work. This will prevent you from getting TM matches for the text that you are currently translating and for any future translations for which you use the TM.

If you have already opened a document for translation in the **Editor** view and want to add a further TM in mid-translation, from the ribbon in the **Editor** view, choose the **Home** tab and then click the **Project Settings** button, as shown in the following screenshot:

The **Project Settings** dialog opens with the **Translation Memory and Automated Translation** setting already showing, so that you can select the TM as described earlier in this section.

Options in the Open Document dialog box

The following table explains the role of each option in the **Open Document** dialog box. In most situations, the options (other than possibly **Update**, if you are working with more than one TM) are left unchanged (that is to say, all the boxes remain checked). All of these options can be configured separately for each TM in the list. You will see how these options work in practice when you go through *Chapter 3, Translating a File*.

Option	Behavior
Enabled	If checked, the TM will be active during translation.
Lookup	If checked, the TM will automatically be searched for matches when you move to a new translation segment.
Penalty	The percentage matches from this TM will be decreased by this number. A penalty of 1, therefore, means that a 100% match is reduced to a 99% match. This is useful to flag 100% matches from a particular TM as requiring extra caution or attention, for example, if you are using a TM created for a different client, in which some of the terminology or expression may be different from that required for the translation that you are currently working on.
Concordance	If checked, you will be able to select strings of text in the translation, and manually search the TM for matches inside stored segments.
Update	If checked, segments will be stored in the TM as you translate.

Working with the translation memories list

To remove a TM from the list, select it in the list of TMs and click **Remove**. This does not delete the TM from your machine. If need be, you can reselect it by clicking **Add** again.

If there are matches of the same level from more than one TM, the result from the highest TM in the list is displayed first in the **Translation Results** window of the **Editor** view while you translate. To move the selected TM up or down the list, use the blue arrow symbols as shown in the following screenshot:

When you open a document for translation via **File** | **Open** | **Translate Single Document** (and if necessary, then select your language pair), the TMs that you used the last time you worked in that language pair will automatically reappear in the list.

Previously used TMs with a different language pair than the one currently selected in the **Open Document** dialog box will appear grayed out in the list, as in the case of the TM at the bottom of the list in the preceding screenshot.

Organizing your translation memories

There are several choices for organizing your TMs, and it is worth taking time to consider what is best for your situation. The central considerations are whether to use fewer and larger, or more and smaller TMs, and how to organize them thematically by, say, assignment, client, or subject matter (or a combination of these).

Concentrating your material in fewer, larger memories may produce more matches, but this should be balanced against factors such as an increased risk of data loss (for example, if a TM is accidentally deleted), possible confidentiality or terminology issues (such as when storing material from several clients in the same TM), and potentially slower searches (in the case of very big TMs).

An example (suggested by Jerzy Czopik, one of the technical reviewers of this book) is that of Microsoft and Apple terminology, where the same source segment may require a different translation depending on the version of the operating system. The word *folder* in English has had several different translations into Polish, depending on the Windows version. In this situation, putting all the content into a single TM with a mix of subjects and customers could cause problems further down the line.

The fact that you can use multiple TMs should also be taken into account, because it allows you simultaneously to use several TMs created for, say, particular clients or subject areas. Furthermore, the fact that you can control the update settings for each TM separately makes it easy to determine which of the active TMs will receive new content as you work.

Summary

In this chapter, you have learned how to create TMs and select them when you open an individual document for translation in SDL Trados Studio. In the next chapter, we will look at how to put your TMs to use in translating a document in SDL Trados Studio.

3
Translating a File

There are two ways to approach the translation of a document in SDL Trados Studio. The one that is discussed in this chapter involves selecting and opening a single document for translation. This is the simplest way to go about translating an individual document. The other is to create a project, which we will discuss in detail in *Chapter 7, Working with Projects*. The latter approach requires slightly more preparation but has several advantages, one of which is the ability to more easily group files for translation, as the project creation process does this for you. You can also retain your translation settings to re-use later, in the form of a project template. Regardless of which approach you use, however, the process of translating your documents in the side-by-side editor, which is the main focus of this chapter, is essentially the same.

In this chapter, we will show you how the process of translating works in SDL Trados Studio, from opening a file to generating the translated document. In between, we look at some practical tips and tricks for getting the best out of SDL Trados Studio while you translate. We will finish the chapter with some ideas for customizing the translation interface in the **Editor** view.

Downloading the sample files

The sample files for use with Chapters 3, 4, 5, and 6 can be downloaded from http://www.packtpub.com. If you purchased this book elsewhere, you can visit http://www.packtpub.com/support and register to have the files e-mailed directly to you.

The Editor view

The **Editor** view is shown in the following screenshot, with the main sections, which we will discuss later in this chapter, highlighted:

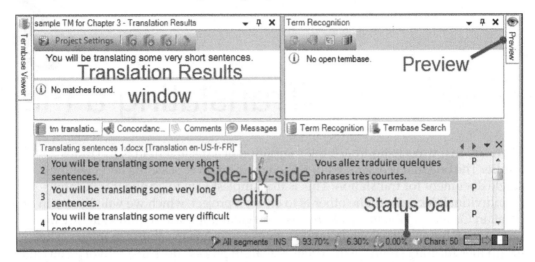

The Editor view ribbon

When you open a document for translation in the **side-by-side editor**, the ribbon in the **Editor** view expands to contain two additional tabs. The **Review** tab contains review-specific commands, discussed in *Chapter 6, Editing and Quality Assurance*. The **Advanced** tab contains a varied collection of commands likely to be used less frequently, such as for changing the case of your text, or locking segments to prevent editing.

 The **Home** tab initially contains only the **Project Settings** button, and the other ribbon groups do not appear until you open a document in the side-by-side editor. The ribbons adjust automatically to include the functions relevant to the main window content.

Translating a file in SDL Trados Studio

This section describes the basic process of opening a document in SDL Trados Studio, translating it, and generating a target file. To work along with the instructions in this section, download Chap_03_SampleFile_01.docx from http://www.packtpub.com/sdl-trados-studio-practical-guide/book.

Opening an individual document for translation

To open a document for translation in SDL Trados Studio, perform the following steps:

1. In any view, choose **File | Open | Translate Single Document** or press *Ctrl + Shift + O*. Browse to the file that you want to open for translation, select it, and click **Open**. In this example we open the sample file `Chap_03_SampleFile_01.docx`.

   Alternatively, you can open a file using drag and drop. You must be in the **Editor** view to do this. Drag the file from Windows Explorer into the Navigation pane, shown in the following screenshot:

2. In the **Open Document** window, shown in the following screenshot, select the desired **Source Language** and **Target Language**. If you are using the sample file, please choose **English (US)** as your source language and a language of your choice as your target language.

3. Select one or more TMs by clicking **Add** and browsing to select an existing TM. You can also choose to create a new TM at this point by clicking **Create** (choose **New File-based Translation Memory**, specify a **Name** and **Location** for the file, and click **Finish**). The process of creating and selecting a TM is described in detail in *Chapter 2, Creating and Using Translation Memories*. If you are working with our sample file, please create or select a TM of your own at this point. The following screenshot shows the **Open Document** window after we add the TM:

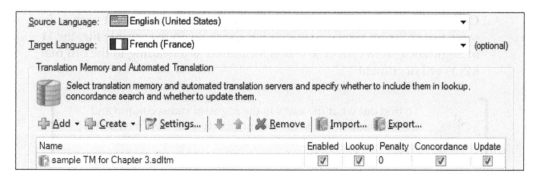

For any other settings, click the **Advanced** button at the bottom-left corner of the window.

4. Click **OK** to open the document for translation in the side-by-side editor.

Translating in the side-by-side editor

The side-by-side editor is made up of five columns, numbered in the following screenshot:

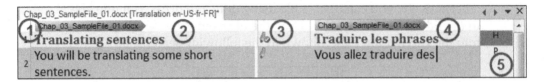

At the top left is a tab showing the name of the active document. The numbers in circles represent the following:

- **Column 1**: The segment number.
- **Column 2**: The source text, divided into segments when you open the file for translation.
- **Column 3**: The segment status and translation origin, indicating what work you have done on each segment at any given point in time, and where the match came from. The icons have the following meanings:

Not translated	Draft	Translated

- **Column 4**: Where you type the translation.
- **Column 5**: Information to indicate the context of each segment within the structure of the original document. For example, in the sample file, the **H** in **Segment 1** shows that the text is formatted as a heading in the original MS Word document.

> To find out what the icons in the segment status column and the information in the document structure column mean, move your mouse pointer over that part of the segment to display a tool tip or click on it for more detailed information.

Translating the text

1. To begin translating, click in the first target segment and type the translation. As soon as you start typing, the status symbol changes from ☐ (Not Translated) to 🖉 (Draft) showing that you have edited the segment but not stored it in the TM yet, as shown in the following screenshot. **Segment 1** of the sample file is a heading, as indicated by the letter **H** on the right. Notice that the visual formatting of the text as displayed by SDL Trados Studio is replicated when you type the translation.

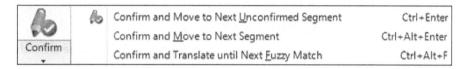

2. When you are happy with your translation, press *Ctrl + Enter* to store the translated segment in the TM and move to the next segment that needs translating (pressing *Enter* alone has no effect). Alternatively, in the **Home** tab, click the **Confirm** button, shown on the left of the following screenshot:

	Confirm and Move to Next Unconfirmed Segment	Ctrl+Enter
Confirm	Confirm and Move to Next Segment	Ctrl+Alt+Enter
	Confirm and Translate until Next Fuzzy Match	Ctrl+Alt+F

This action is generally described as *confirming* the segment. The status symbol changes from 🖉 (Draft), to 🖉 (Translated) to indicate that the segment has been confirmed. Segments that you translate or edit must be confirmed in this way, or they will not be stored in the TM.

The default confirm action (*Ctrl + Enter*) actually moves you to the next unconfirmed segment, skipping any confirmed segments in between. To show more options for confirming segments, as shown in the preceding screenshot, click the drop-down arrow under the **Confirm** button.

To go to the next segment down, whether confirmed or not, choose **Confirm and Move to Next Segment** (*Ctrl + Alt + Enter*). If you are translating a file that produces lots of 100% matches that you do not wish to check immediately, choose **Confirm and Translate until Next Fuzzy Match** (*Ctrl + Alt + F*). You will then move down the bilingual file, automatically confirming any 100% matches, and only stopping at the next match that is less than 100%.

3. Now translate and confirm **Segment 2**. This moves you into **Segment 3**, which is a fuzzy or partial match as indicated by the figure 82% in the following screenshot:

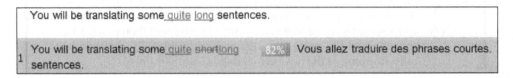

Typing accented characters

The ability to type accented characters in SDL Trados Studio is dependent on the keyboard settings in MS Windows, as with any other application that you might run on MS Windows. If you are using an English language keyboard and want to type accented characters in the target segment, you can use the *Alt* codes (such as *Alt* + 0233 for é). It is also possible to change the keyboard to follow the target language layout, via the **Control Panel** in MS Windows.

The Translation Results window

Whenever you move into a new segment (as from **Segment 2** to **Segment 3**), the TM (or TMs if more than one is active) is searched for matches, and the highest match appears in the target segment (this action is called *Lookup*). If a match is found, the results are displayed in the **Translation Results** window, and an icon appears in the segment status column in the side-by-side editor to show the match level. By default, if no matches are found, the target segment remains empty, and the **Translation Results** window displays the text **No matches found**.

The **Translation Results** window displays the text in the current segment in the white area at the top, and any match from the TM underneath it, as shown in the following screenshot. The blue and red text in the source segment indicates the words that need to be added to and deleted from the new segment compared to the match from the TM (in a similar form to that used in **Track Changes** in MS Word). In this case, for example, we need to add **quite long** and delete **short** in the translation.

Edit the target segment to make the translation correct, and then confirm. When you edit and confirm the segment, the fuzzy match icon changes to a transparent background, as shown in the following screenshot. Notice that the fuzzy match value remains even after you confirm the segment. Thus, the percentage values displayed always indicate the value of the match as *originally* offered by the TM (the **translation origin**).

Inserting matches from the TM

The following screenshot shows the sample file before we edit and confirm **Segment 4**:

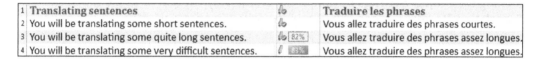

Each match in the **Translation Results** window has a number, as shown on the left of the following screenshot. As you will see when you get to **Segment 4** (which we will now edit and confirm), the highest match (with the number **1** in the column on the left) is automatically inserted whenever you move into an empty target segment.

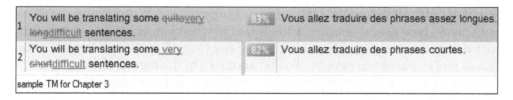

To insert a different match instead, press *Ctrl* and the numbers on the main keyboard. For example, to insert match number 2, press *Ctrl + 2*.

To insert the match currently highlighted in blue in the **Translation Results** window, click the **Apply Translation** button or choose **Home | Apply Translation** (*Ctrl + T*). You can also scroll the list of matches to insert other matches via the **Select Previous Match** (*Alt + PgUp*) and **Select Next Match** (*Alt + PgDn*) buttons.

Notice that the yellow bar at the bottom of the **Translation Results** window shows the name of the TM providing the match in the segment that is highlighted in blue, as in the preceding screenshot.

No matches from your TM?

If you are not getting matches from your TM, look at the **Translation Results** window. The text **No matches found** indicates that there is an enabled TM. If you see this text, the problem could simply be that there is no match for the segment. It could also be that you forgot to confirm the preceding segments (and thereby store them in the TM) when you translated them. Alternatively, it could be that the TM is not set to update, and has therefore not stored any of the translations that you have confirmed up to this point.

The text **No open translation memories or automated translation servers**, on the other hand, means that no TM is enabled or selected for use.

To correct these problems during translation, you can modify the TM options by clicking the **Project Settings** button in the **Home** view ribbon or at the top of the **Translation Results** window, shown in the following screenshot:

The option **Translation Memory and Automated Translation** is selected by default. Here, you can at any point add, remove, or create memories, and change the settings for those you are already using.

Using more than one TM

We discussed how to add another, additional TM when you open a document for translation in the section in *Chapter 2, Creating and Using Translation Memories*, titled *Adding a further translation memory*. To add another TM during translation, from the **Home** view, click **Project Settings**. Under the option **Translation Memory and Automated Translation**, follow the instructions in *Chapter 2, Creating and Using Translation Memories*, (if you are working along with our sample file, it is not necessary to add a further TM to complete the exercise in this chapter).

When you use more than one TM during translation, the white bar at the top of the **Translation Results** window displays the names of the TMs being used (in the order in which they appear in the TM list), as shown in the following screenshot:

Editing a confirmed segment

To edit a confirmed segment, simply click in the target cell and edit the text. Try this in one of the confirmed **Segments 1** to **3**. As soon as you start editing, the status symbol will change from **Translated** to **Draft**. When you confirm the segment by pressing *Ctrl + Enter*, the edited version of your translation will replace the version existing in any TMs that are set to update. To check this, move back into the segment you have just edited and confirmed; the **Translation Results** window will show the updated segment in the TM.

> You do not necessarily have to translate the segments in order. Click in any segment in the document to translate or edit it, or use the arrow keys to move up and down the bilingual file without confirming the segments as you go.

Clearing the target segment

To clear the target cell and start the translation afresh, in the **Home** tab, click the **Clear Target Segment** button, shown in the following screenshot:

Tracking your progress

The progress bar at the bottom right shows your progress through the document in terms of the status indicators, updated in real time as you translate. The following screenshot shows the situation after we confirm **Segment 4** and begin typing **Segment 5** in the sample file. The current number of characters in the target segment is shown on the right-hand side.

By double-clicking the status bar, you can choose to show the word count as well as the percentage (since the word count will often be a more useful indicator of your progress).

For another useful graphical representation of your current progress, go to the **Files** view and, at the bottom left, click the **Confirmation Statistics** tab.

Saving your bilingual document

It is advisable to save your bilingual file frequently during translation. Here, we will save and close the sample file, and then reopen it to continue with the translation.

1. To save the bilingual file for the first time, choose **File | Save**, click the **Save** button in the **Quick Access Toolbar** at the top right, or press *Ctrl + S*.

2. You are then prompted to choose a location to save the bilingual file (which is, by default, normally the folder that you last selected). Choose a folder where you want to save the bilingual file; for example, in the same folder as your original file.

 If you are working in a project, as described later in *Chapter 7, Working with Projects*, source and target folders are automatically created in the project folder. The bilingual file is automatically created in both. When you save the bilingual file, it is by default saved in the target folder.

3. As shown in the following screenshot, SDL Trados Studio automatically gives the file a name in three parts: the name of the original document and its file extension, the language pair, and the bilingual file extension `.sdlxliff`.

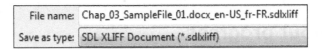

File name:	Chap_03_SampleFile_01.docx_en-US_fr-FR.sdlxliff
Save as type:	SDL XLIFF Document (*.sdlxliff)

4. Click **Save** to save your bilingual file.

 Changing the suggested filename is generally not necessary or advisable. SDL Trados Studio always names files in this way to make them easy to identify. This can help you keep track of your files and maintain order on your computer.

An asterisk after the filename at the top of the side-by-side editor indicates that you have not saved the file since you last edited it, as shown in the following screenshot:

Chap_03_SampleFile_01.docx_en-US_fr-FR.sdlxliff [Translation]*

The asterisk disappears whenever you save the file.

The SDL Trados Studio file in which you do your translation is usually referred to as a *bilingual file* or SDLXLIFF. The SDLXLIFF is not created until you save the bilingual file in the side-by-side editor for the first time. If you exit the side-by-side editor without saving the file at least once, no SDLXLIFF is created, and you will lose any work that you have done in the SDLXLIFF to that point.

Once you save your SDLXLIFF, your folder will contain two files, the SDLXLIFF (with a green and gold icon) and an sdlproj file (with a blue icon), as shown in the following screenshot:

The sdlproj file is a **project file** created automatically by SDL Trados Studio when you save an SDLXLIFF for the first time. You can simply leave it your folder. The sdlproj file contains information about settings such as which TMs you are using, and ensures that the SDLXLIFF uses those same settings whenever you reopen it.

AutoSave

Like Microsoft Word, SDL Trados Studio automatically saves your document at regular intervals. When you reopen a document that crashed with unsaved changes, you are prompted to recover the last AutoSaved file, which overwrites the original SDLXLIFF document. The **AutoSave** interval can be changed under **File** | **Options** | **Editor**, at the bottom of the dialog box (the default **AutoSave** interval is every 10 minutes).

Closing and reopening a bilingual file

Let us assume that you need to stop translating at this point for some reason, with a view to resuming later. To close an SDLXLIFF document in the **Editor** view (remembering to save it first), click the **Close Document (X)** button at the top right of the side-by-side window, or choose **File** | **Close** (*Ctrl + F4*).

It is possible to reopen a saved SDLXLIFF to resume translation in the **Editor** by choosing **Translate Single Document** and browsing to select the SDLXLIFF (not the original document). However, there is a more convenient method.

The project file created by SDL Trados Studio when you first save your document has the same name as that of your SDLXLIFF, and stays in the list of projects in the **Projects** view even when you close and reopen SDL Trados Studio. This provides an easy way to reopen individual SDLXLIFF documents.

To reopen your document and resume translation, go to the **Projects** view and select the corresponding project name, and then go to the **Files** view (alternatively, double-click the project name in the **Projects** view to jump straight to the **Files** view). In the **Files** view, you can open your SDLXLIFF document in the **Editor** by double-clicking it or, from the ribbon, choosing **Open For Translation**.

If you do not see your project in the **Projects** view, choose **File | Open | Open Project** and open the sdlproj file, and then follow the instructions in the preceding paragraph to open the SDLXLIFF.

If you do not have the sdlproj file, you can open the SDLXLIFF in the **Editor** view by selecting it via **File | Open | Translate Single Document**. This is useful if you receive an SDLXLIFF file from someone else for proofreading, for example.

We will now go on to translate the rest of the sample file.

Concordance – searching inside the TM

Segments 5 and 6 both contain the phrase **idiomatic expressions**, but the segments as a whole are not similar enough to produce a match from the TM. When you translate and confirm **Segment 5**, there is no match from the TM for **Segment 6**. However, you can still access your translation of any chunk of text by searching the TM for segments (both source and target) in which it occurs. This process is called **concordance**.

To run a concordance search in the side-by-side editor (in our example, to search for the text **idiomatic expressions** in **Segment 6**), perform the following steps:

1. Select the relevant text in the source or target segment in the side-by-side editor and press *F3*. Alternatively, click the **Concordance Search** tab above the side-by-side editor window, shown in the following screenshot, with the name of the TM:

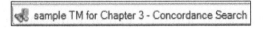

2. Paste or type in the text, and choose **Search Source** or **Search Target** from the dropdown next to the search field (shown in the following screenshot).

You can also run concordance searches from the ribbon. Select the text to search, and in the **Home** tab, choose **Concordance Search** and then **Source Concordance Search** (*Ctrl* + *F3*) or **Target Concordance Search** (*Ctrl* + *Shift* + *F3*).

The results are highlighted in yellow, as shown in the following screenshot:

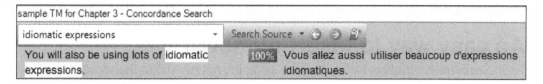

To insert the translation in your target segment, perform the following steps:

1. In the side-by-side editor, click at the insertion point in the target segment.
2. In the **Concordance Search** window, select the relevant target text.
3. Right-click and choose **Insert into document** (or press *Ctrl* + *Alt* + *F3*), as shown in the following screenshot. If the **Insert into document** option is grayed out, ensure that you have clicked in your target segment and try again. Alternatively, copy and paste the translation into your target segment.

Automatic concordance searches

If there is no match from the TM, SDL Trados Studio will attempt to search the TM for source segments containing chunks of text toward the beginning of the source segment in the document. The automatic concordance search option is not enabled by default. To enable it, go to **File** | **Options**. Under **Editor** | **Concordance Search Window**, check the option **Perform search if the TM lookup returns no results**.

In **Segment 7**, there is no match from the TM, but the automatic concordance search finds a TM segment containing **idiomatic expressions**, as shown in the following screenshot. The figure of **50%** indicates the overall TM match for the segment. You can practice this technique again later in the sample file when you get to **Segment 11**.

You will also notice that **Segment 15** has been completed further down the SDLXLIFF, a point to which we return in the next section.

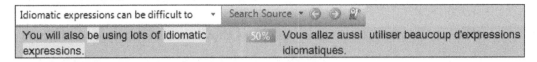

An easy way to insert numbers

As in **Segment 8**, numbers (when written as digits, not words) in the source segment have a blue underline. Blue-underlined elements are deemed by SDL Trados Studio to be non-translatable elements, or **placeables**, which are ready to be *placed* in the target segment without translation. Instead of typing or copying and pasting a number, you can insert it by pressing *Ctrl + ,*. This technique is called **QuickPlace**.

When you press *Ctrl + ,* the digit is highlighted in the source segment and a QuickPlace list opens with the digits in the segment, shown on the right-hand side of the following screenshot:

Select the digit in the list with your mouse or arrow keys (the highlighting in the source segment now moves to reflect your selection). Press *Enter* to insert the number in the target segment. The number is also presented in the convention used in the target language (here, in the French translation, the thousands are separated by a space instead of a comma).

 Other examples of placeables are markup and formatting tags, dates, and acronyms, all of which can be inserted by pressing *Ctrl + ,*.

Auto-propagating segments

Auto-propagation is the automatic completion of other matching segments in the SDLXLIFF when a segment is confirmed. If you confirm a segment that is repeated in target segments further down the SDLXLIFF, the 100% match is inserted into those segments automatically.

It is advisable to check and confirm auto-propagated segments with *Ctrl + Enter*, so that you will know subsequently that you have finished working on the segment.

In the sample file, when you confirmed **Segment 7**, **Segment 15** was auto-propagated as a 100% match, as shown in the following screenshot. You can check and confirm it when you reach that point in the file.

You can configure auto-propagation to behave in various ways, discussed in depth in *Chapter 6, Editing and Quality Assurance*.

Auto-propagated 100% matches with placeables

By default, when a segment is auto-propagated to another segment whose content is identical except for any placeables, a 100% match results.

When you confirm **Segment 9**, **Segment 10** is auto-propagated with an unconfirmed 100% match, and the digits **80,000** (in our example, in the French number format) are substituted in the target, as shown in the following screenshot:

Notice that when you confirm **Segment 10**, color and shading of the 100% match icon does not change, so that you will know when you review your work later that the match was originally auto-propagated, as shown in the following screenshot:

>
>
> **Auto-localization penalty**
>
> In most situations, auto-propagating 100% matches does not cause problems, but you may sometimes prefer to trigger a 99% match instead to give you a stronger reminder to check the translation of auto-propagated segments containing numbers and other placeables that are auto-substituted in this way. To do this, from the **Home** tab, choose **Project Settings**. The window opens with the option **Translation Memory and Automated Translation** already selected. Under **Penalties**, change the percentage under **Auto-localization penalty** from 0 to 1. For more information on penalties, see the SDL help pages at http://tinyurl.com/tm-penalties.

Standard Windows shortcuts

Many standard Windows shortcuts will work in SDL Trados Studio (for example, *Ctrl + Z* (undo), *Shift + F3* (change case), and *Ctrl + B* (bold). In **Segment 11**, copy and paste the translation of **idiomatic expressions** (or find it using concordance).

Splitting and merging segments

In some situations, the match levels obtained from the TM can be improved by changing the way the document is segmented in the side-by-side editor.

Splitting a segment into two

Segment 12 is clearly two statements in one, as shown in the following screenshot:

| 12 | There are lots of these to translate Idiomatic expressions are all over the place |

To split it into two, click at the point in the source segment at which you want to split the segment (in our example, before the word **Idiomatic**), then right-click and choose **Split Segment** (*Alt + Shift + T*). The split segments are assigned new segment numbers, in our case **12a** and **12b**, as shown in the following screenshot, so that the numbering of the segments further down the SDLXLIFF is unaffected.

| 12a | There are lots of these to translate |
| 12b | Idiomatic expressions are all over the place |

Adding line breaks inside segments

You can add soft returns (line breaks within the same paragraph) inside the target segment. To add a soft return, place your mouse pointer at the right point in the target segment and press *Shift + Enter*. The following screenshot shows target **Segment 12** with a soft return at the end of the first line:

| ∅ | Il·y·en·a·beaucoup·à·traduire. ↵ |
| | Les·expressions·idiomatiques·sont·partout. |

This also creates an equivalent soft return in the translated document when it is generated.

To display whitespace information such as soft returns, in the **Home** view click the **Show Whitespace Characters** button, shown in the following screenshot:

Editing the source segment

It is possible to edit the source segment in SDLXLIFF files based on .doc (MS Word 2000-2003), .docx, .ppt (Microsoft PowerPoint XP-2003), and .pptx files. In the **Home** tab, choose **Project Settings | Project**, then activate the option **Allow source editing for supported file types**. To edit the text, right-click in the active source segment and choose **Edit Source** (*Alt + F2*). In the sample file, in **Segment 16**, the two words are joined together, so we can edit the segment to add a space, as shown in the following screenshot:

16 Complicated sentences

Source editing is disabled in certain circumstances, such as for documents that contain tracked changes in the source (for details, see the SDL help pages at http://tinyurl.com/edit-source).

Multiple translations of the same source segment

To add a translation to the TM as an alternative translation alongside the existing target segment in the TM (instead of overwriting it), from the **Advanced** tab, choose **Add as New Translation** (*Ctrl + Shift + U*) and then press *Ctrl + Enter*. In the sample file, we add an alternative translation for **Segment 16**.

If there is more than one translation in the TM for the same source segment, a multiple translations penalty is applied, reducing the match level by **1%** to **99%** (indicated by the green plus icon underneath the match percentage). To see this, move back into **Segment 16** and look at the **Translation Results** window, shown in the following screenshot:

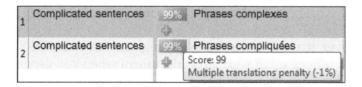

Penalties are there to prompt you to reflect on whether or not you should accept the first match that you are being offered. If a match is 100%, you are perhaps less likely to consider the alternatives before accepting. It is possible to adjust the level of the penalties that you apply by going to **Project Settings**, as with the **Auto-localization penalty** described earlier in this chapter.

Merging two or more consecutive segments

Select the first of the segments. To select the subsequent segments, hold the *Ctrl* key down and click in the segment number column on the left of the side-by-side editor so that the background color of the subsequent segments becomes yellow, as shown in the following screenshot, in which **Segments 13 and 14** will be merged:

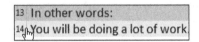

Now right-click and choose **Merge Segments** (*Ctrl + Alt + S*).

Merging segments over hard returns

SDL Trados Studio does not let you merge segments over hard returns created in the original document. However, source segment editing provides a workaround; that is, by editing two source segments, you can cut and paste text from one to the other.

Segments 17 and 18 in the sample file are separated by a hard return in the sample Word document, and the **Merge Segments** command will not work. As shown in the following screenshot, we can get round this by editing the source segments to cut and paste the text from **Segment 18** to **Segment 17**. To do this, first in **Segment 18**, we choose **Edit Source** (*Alt + F2*), select the text in the segment, and copy it to the clipboard with the **Cut** command (*Ctrl + X*). Then, in **Segment 17**, we choose **Edit Source** again, and paste in the text from **Segment 18** at the end of the segment. In our sample file, the combined segment now produces a **100%** match, as shown in the following screenshot:

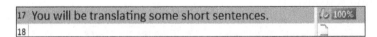

Be aware, however, that this can leave empty segments in your SDLXLIFF file, which may need tidying up in your target document when you generate it later.

On occasion, this approach can prevent you from generating the target file, so it is a good idea to check that you are able to save the target file before making extensive changes (see the section later in this chapter titled *Generating the translated document*). If you cannot generate the target document with an empty source segment like this, you can leave some dummy text (such as ?????) in the source segment, as long as you remember to remove it from the target file later. Do not confirm such segments, as they contain no meaningful text.

For segments that are unlikely to appear in this form again in a future document, an alternative is to translate the segments without confirming them, as shown in the following screenshot. The translated text will appear on separate lines when you generate your target document, but the TM will not be cluttered up with unhelpful text fragments.

| 17 | You will be translating | | Vous allez traduire |
| 18 | some short sentences. | | des phrases courtes. |

Customizing the keyboard shortcuts

The keyboard shortcuts in SDL Trados Studio can be customized. You can add a new keyboard shortcut for a particular action or change the existing ones. However, you will need to know the name of the action to which you are assigning a new keyboard shortcut, so check this information in the SDL Trados Studio interface before you proceed.

As an example, we will add a shortcut for switching to **Alternative Translation Layout**, which has none assigned by default. Choose **File | Options | Keyboard Shortcuts**. In the list of shortcuts, under **Editor**, find the row containing **Alternative Translation Layout** and click in the **Shortcut** column. On your keyboard, press the desired shortcut key combination (such as *Ctrl + Shift + Q*), then click **OK** to exit the **Options** dialog box.

If you choose a shortcut that is already in use, it will be displayed in red to indicate that the shortcut is not available. Place your mouse pointer over the red area to see a tool tip telling you what action that shortcut is assigned to, as shown in the following screenshot:

| Alternative Translation Layout | Ctrl+Shift+N | |
| Analysis Statistics | | Shortcut already in use by Editor > Add Comment |

In this case, to revert from **Alternative Translation Layout** to the standard layout, press the new shortcut again.

Standard formatting and special characters

The **Formatting** and **QuickInsert** groups (shown in the following screenshot) sit in the **Home** tab and feature a number of buttons for inserting standard formatting (such as bold and underlining) and special characters (such as €, ©, and ™):

To display the corresponding keyboard shortcut, place your mouse pointer over the icon.

To insert individual symbols such as €, place your mouse pointer at the right point in the target segment and click the symbol in the ribbon. To insert formatting such as quotation marks around some text, as in the following screenshot from **Segment 19**, in the target segment, select the text and then click the appropriate quotation mark button:

Automated translation

As in **Segment 21** (you can translate **Segment 20** first), SDL Trados Studio will attempt to translate automatically segments that contain only placeables (such as URLs or numbers), giving the segment the translation origin icon **AT**, shown in the following screenshot:

| 21 | 0316112013 | | AT | 0316112013 |

The same icon is used to indicate matches from any automated translation providers, such as **SDL BeGlobal**, that you have chosen to use.

Previewing your translation

The **Preview** feature allows you to preview during translation how your document will look in the finished version and to see your translations in their final document context. The default mode, **Real-time Preview**, refreshes every time you confirm a segment.

To see a preview of your work, on the right of the side-by-side editor, hover your mouse pointer over the **Preview** tab. The **Preview** window is set to auto-hide, so it will slide out when you do this. Click the link **Click here to generate initial preview**.

When you select a segment in the side-by-side editor, the corresponding segment is selected in the **Preview** window, as shown in the following screenshot, and vice versa:

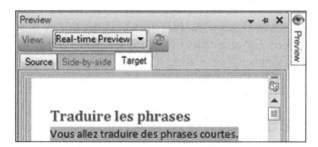

To resize the **Preview** window, drag its left edge to the left. If the preview text is too small, you can change the view options at the bottom of the **Preview** window, as shown in the following screenshot:

If you are working with a large document and the **Real-time Preview** becomes slow, change the **View** option at the top of the **Preview** window to **Preview**. You can now update the **Preview** as you work by clicking the refresh button or pressing *Ctrl + R*.

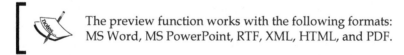
The preview function works with the following formats: MS Word, MS PowerPoint, RTF, XML, HTML, and PDF.

To leave the **Preview** window open while you work, click the **Auto Hide** button so that it points down (see the section titled *Customizing the Editor view*, later in this chapter).

Generating the translated document

This section explains how to produce a translation in the same format as the original file once you have finished translating your document in SDL Trados Studio. Do this with the sample file to complete the translation exercise for this chapter:

1. To generate the translated version of a document open in the side-by-side editor (ensuring that you have first saved it in SDLXLIFF format), choose **File | Save Target As** or press *Shift + F12*.

2. The **Save Target As** dialog box will prompt you to save the translated document in the same folder and with the same name as the source document. This will of course overwrite the source document with the translated document.

You may therefore wish to change the filename and the folder in which you save the translated document, for example, by saving the translated document in a separate target files folder and/or adding a suffix to the filename to indicate that is the translation.

AutoSuggest technologies

At a basic level, the set of features collectively named **AutoSuggest** is similar to the **AutoComplete** feature in MS Word in that it automatically offers possible matches (suggestions) for words or strings of text as you type. There are three possible sources of AutoSuggest matches: **AutoText**, **AutoSuggest dictionaries**, and **MultiTerm termbases** (MultiTerm termbases are covered in *Chapter 8, Managing Terminology*). The following screenshot shows AutoSuggest matches being produced simultaneously from a termbase and an AutoSuggest dictionary:

AutoSuggest speeds up the process of typing and translating by offering matches on strings of text *inside* segments, as opposed to the *segment-level* matches offered by the TM, and can be used in conjunction with a TM.

AutoText

AutoText is a feature for completing words as you type. You first specify the words or strings of text that you want to match against. SDL Trados Studio then offers them as suggestions to choose from as you type.

- **To add a word or string of text to the AutoText list**: Select the text that you want to add in the target segment. From the **Advanced** tab, click **Add AutoText** (*Alt + F7*). Click **Add** to add your string to the list. Click **OK** to exit the **Options** dialog box.

- **To insert an AutoText match as you type**: As you type the first four letters, any corresponding AutoText entries will appear in a list, as shown in the following screenshot:

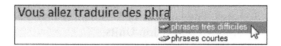

In the list, use your mouse or the arrow keys to select the best match. Hit the *Enter* key or double-click to insert the match into your target segment.

AutoSuggest dictionaries

An AutoSuggest dictionary is, like a TM, a *database* to help you while you translate. However, in contrast to a TM, an AutoSuggest dictionary has the following features:

- It gets generated in its completed form before you start translation.

- It does not get updated or changed in anyway during the translation.

- It provides matches for strings of text inside the segment as you type.

- It produces context-sensitive matches. For example, if you type the letters exc, only the matches in the AutoSuggest dictionary beginning with those letters and relevant to the content of the segment will appear as suggestions.

Users of the Freelance version can open and use AutoSuggest dictionaries, but must buy the AutoSuggest Creator add-on to create their own, so the **Generate AutoSuggest Dictionary** option is unavailable in the Freelance version.

Try searching the web for ready-made AutoSuggest dictionaries made freely available by others, some of which can be downloaded from the SDL site at http://tinyurl.com/autosuggest-dictionary. You might also try creating them out of the European Union translation memories.

Generating an AutoSuggest dictionary

AutoSuggest dictionaries are generated from existing TM in SDL Trados Studio
(.sdltm) or .tmx format. To generate an AutoSuggest dictionary, you must have
a TM in one of these formats that contains at least 10,000 translation units (TUs).

To see the number of TUs in a TM, in the **Translation Memories**
view, from the **Home** tab, click **Open**. Once selected, your TM will
appear in the list at the top left. Right-click the name of the TM and
choose **Settings**. The number of TUs is shown at the bottom of the
dialog box under **Translation Units**.

The main things you need to know about AutoSuggest dictionaries are as follows:

- **To generate an AutoSuggest dictionary**: Go to the **Translation Memories**
  view. In the **Home** tab, choose **Create AutoSuggest Dictionary** and follow
  the instructions in the wizard.

- **To select an AutoSuggest dictionary for use during translation**: Choose
  Project Settings | Language Pairs. Under the appropriate language pair,
  choose **AutoSuggest Dictionaries**. On the right, click **Add**, then select
  the AutoSuggest dictionary and click **Open**. Click **OK** to exit the **Project
  Settings** screen. You can also add an AutoSuggest Dictionary when using
  the **Translate Single Document** command. To do so, click the **Advanced**
  button in the **Open Document** window where you add TMs before you
  start translating.

- **To insert an AutoSuggest dictionary match as you type**: The AutoSuggest
  dictionary will produce context-sensitive matches as you type, with the
  first letters of corresponding entries appearing in a list, as shown in the
  following screenshot:

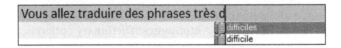

In the list, use your mouse or the arrow keys to select the best match. Press
the *Enter* key or double-click to insert the match into your target segment.
The list is circular, so if there are lots of entries, you can reach the last entry
quickly by going up rather than down.

Customizing the Editor view

This section describes various ways to adapt the **Editor** view to your own way
of working. The **View** tab contains a number of features for modifying the display,
which appear in three separate groups, shown together in the following screenshot,
when a document is open in the Editor:

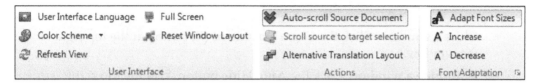

Try experimenting with the following changes to discover what works best for you:

- **Return to the default window layout**: When adjusting the layout as
  described in the rest of this section, you can return to the default window
  layout stored in your profile at any time by choosing **View | Reset Window
  Layout**. You can therefore experiment without fear!

- **Enter Full Screen mode**: Press *F11* or choose **Full Screen** to enter and exit
  Full Screen mode, where the screen space given to the side-by-side editor
  is maximized.

- **Position the side-by-side editor higher up**: Choose **Alternative Translation
  Layout** to move the side-by-side editor above the **Translation Results** and
  other windows. To return to the standard layout, click the command again.

- **Adjust the font sizes**: To adjust the font sizes of the source and target text
  in the side-by-side editor, in the **View** tab, choose **Adapt Font Sizes**, then
  Increase or **Decrease**, shown on the right of the preceding screenshot. This
  does not affect the font sizes in your translated document. By choosing **File
  | Options | Editor**, and then **Font Adaption**, you can set maximum and
  minimum source and target font sizes individually.

  You can also adjust the font sizes in the **Translation Results** and **Concordance
  Search** windows by choosing **File | Options | Editor** and then **Translation
  Results Window** or **Concordance Search Window** respectively.

- **Change the way source and target segments scroll**: By default, the source
  and target segments move up and down in tandem when you scroll. To
  decouple them so that you can move one column up and down without
  moving the other, choose **Auto-scroll Source Document**. Click **Auto-scroll
  Source Document** again to recouple them.

- **Resize a window**: Click the edge of the window until your cursor changes to the cross-wire shape and then drag horizontally or vertically, as shown in the following screenshot, in which we drag the top edge of the side-by-side editor up or down.

- **Close a window**: Click the **Close Document (X)** button at the top right of the window.

- **Auto-hide a window**: Click the **Auto Hide** button at the top right of the window so that the pin symbol points to the left. The window displays when you move your mouse pointer over its title bar, and hides itself when inactive.

- **Move a dockable window**: You can move dockable windows to a floating (undocked) position on your screen (or onto another screen), or dock them in a different place. Left-click the title bar of the window and move it. To leave the window floating, release the mouse button at the desired location. To dock the window, wait until the direction indicators appear, as shown in the following screenshot. Drag the window until your mouse pointer is over the direction arrow indicating the desired location (the new position of the window is highlighted in blue), and then release the mouse button.

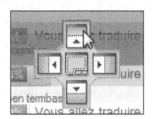

Summary

In this chapter, you learned the basic process of translating a document in SDL Trados Studio and how to produce your translation in the original document format ready to send to your client. We also covered the creation and use of various tools and resources designed to make your translation work more efficient and consistent along the way. In the next chapter, we look in detail at how to use tags to preserve the look and functionality of your document when you translate in SDL Trados Studio.

4
Formatting and Tags

This chapter explains how to ensure that the formatting and functionality of your translated document is the same as that of the original. SDL Trados Studio uses tags to retain information about the formatting (such as bold text) and functionality (such as hyperlinks) in your document. You can, if you wish, download the sample file from the Packt website to work along with the instructions in this chapter.

You may not always be able to tell what the tags are there for, but the golden rule is to add any tags in the source segment at the equivalent position in the target.

By default, SDL Trados Studio shows all recognized formatting in "visual" form without tags. For example, bold or italic text is displayed as bold or italic text and not as unformatted text with tags. Nevertheless, the tags are present in the text, but hidden. Functionality such as hyperlinks, on the other hand, appears in the source segment with the tags displayed. The following screenshot shows a source segment that contains both visual formatting (bold on the word **publications**) and text displayed with tags (around the word **website**) to represent its hyperlink functionality:

For more **publications**, see our hyperlink website hyperlink .

When you translate, the formatting of your target text will initially be different from that of the source. Unless you apply the formatting and functionality of the source to the target, the document will look and behave differently to the source when you produce the target version after translation. In this chapter, we describe how to apply formatting and functionality to your target text to prevent such a situation from arising.

Different formatting penalty

When the text content of a segment produces a 100% match against the TM but the source segments in the document and in the TM contain different formatting, a penalty is applied to the match. In the sample file, **Segments 1 and 2** are the same, except that **Segment 2** contains some text in bold. When you reach **Segment 2**, the **Translation Results** window shows the following match:

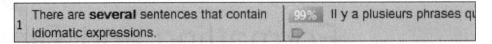

The yellow arrow symbol under the match percentage tells you that a **Different formatting penalty** has been applied. This alerts you to the need to edit the match to ensure that the formatting is consistent in your source and target segments. SDL Trados Studio also has a **Missing format penalty** that would have been triggered if the bold formatting were in **Segment 1** and not in **Segment 2**.

 This different formatting and other penalties are set collectively on the TMs in use. To adjust them, in the **Home** view, choose **Project Settings | Language Pairs | All Language Pairs | Translation Memory and Automated Translation | Penalties**.

Inserting formatting

The quickest way to add formatting and tags is to use **QuickPlace** (*Ctrl + ,*). In the following screenshot, we add the bold formatting in **Segment 2** by selecting the word **plusieurs**, pressing *Ctrl + ,* and then pressing *Enter* to format the selected text:

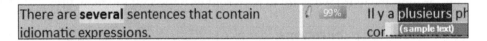

Segment 3, shown in the following screenshot, contains three words that require formatting (in bold, italics, and underline respectively). We type the translation of the entire segment first and then apply the formatting. This is often the easiest way to work with formatting.

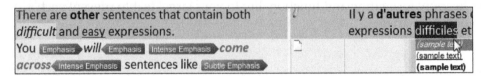

To add the bold formatting to the French word for **other**, we select its translation (**d'autres**) in the target segment and press *Ctrl + ,*. This displays a **QuickPlace list** containing all three instances of formatting in the segment. The currently selected formatting is highlighted in yellow in the source segment. As you move up and down the QuickPlace list, the yellow highlighting also moves to show you which piece of source segment formatting is going to be applied.

To apply the desired formatting to the highlighted text in the target segment, select it in the QuickPlace list and press the *Enter* key. In our example, bold is now applied to the word **d'autres**. When you highlight the next piece of text for formatting in the target segment and press *Ctrl + ,*, the corresponding formatting automatically moves to the top of the QuickPlace list and gets highlighted in the source segment, as shown in the following screenshot:

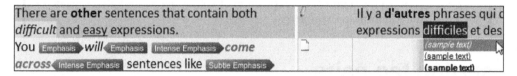

Inserting and working with tags

There are two standard ways to insert tags: using QuickPlace or with mouse and keyboard only.

Inserting single tags

To insert a single tag such as that representing a footnote in the following screenshot:

- **QuickPlace method**: Place your mouse pointer at the insertion point in the target segment and press *Ctrl + ,* to display a QuickPlace formatting list. Select the appropriate tag in the QuickPlace list and press *Enter* to insert it in the target segment, as described in the earlier section titled *Inserting formatting*. This example is from **Segment 4** of the sample file. The footnote text itself appears in **Segment 5**.

The tag currently selected in the QuickPlace list changes to a darker color in the source segment to show you that the tag is currently selected for insertion in the target segment.

- **Mouse method**: Click in the target segment at the insertion point, then hold down the *Ctrl* key and click the relevant tag in the source segment.

  Note that, in addition to the methods described in this section, you can also copy and paste single tags from source to target.

As a general rule, you should ensure that any tags that you insert have the same number of spaces around them in the source and target segments (although you may come across situations when this does not apply, such as when word order differences between source and target require that you place the tag in a different position in the target). In the preceding screenshot, for example, the footnote tag is preceded immediately by the word **sentences** and not by a space. SDL Trados Studio will tend to alert you to spacing errors when you confirm the segment if the position of spaces before and after tags is not identical to the source.

Inserting tag pairs

Tags often work in pairs surrounding a piece of text, with an opening tag pointing right to indicate the start point of the formatting or functionality and a closing tag pointing left to indicate its end, as shown in the hyperlink formatting in the following screenshot from **Segment 6**:

The methods used to insert a single tag can also be used to insert a tag pair, as follows:

- **QuickPlace method**: When using QuickPlace to insert tags in a pair, first type the translation in the target segment and then select it. With the text selected, press *Ctrl + ,*. Select the tag pair from the QuickPlace list, referring to the highlighting in the source segment to ensure that the appropriate tag pair is selected, as shown in the following screenshot. Press *Enter* to insert the tag pair around the text.

- **Mouse method**: First type the translation in the target segment and select the text to be included in the tags. Hold down the *Ctrl* key and click anywhere in the relevant tag pair and text combination in the source segment to insert the tags around the selected text and thereby format it to match the source.

Displaying information about tags

The **Tag Display Mode** buttons in the **View** tab (shown in the following screenshot) allow you to display different levels of detail about what the tags represent. The default setting, selected here, is **Partial Tag Text**:

The bigger the diamond symbol, the more information about the tag is displayed. The following screenshot shows the tag pair in **Segment 6** with the **Full Tag Text** button selected, which displays more detailed information about the hyperlink:

The **No Tag Text** option can also be used to reduce the space taken up by the tags. We discuss the **Tag Id** setting on the right-hand side of the previous screenshot showing the **Tag Display Mode** buttons in the next sections.

Displaying Tag Id numbers

The **Tag Id** setting is useful when it is difficult to work out which tags go where in a segment, as may be the case in **Segment 8**. The **Tag Id** setting switches the display of the tags to an ID number unique to each individual tag or tag pair. This makes it easier to identify which tags are part of the same pair and apply them to the corresponding target text, as in the following screenshot, which shows part of **Segment 8** with the tag IDs displayed:

There are many 11 websites 11 that contain 12 hyperlinks 12 to other 13 *pages* 13 and various other 14

Dealing with tag-heavy segments

Segment 8, shown in the following screenshot, contains many tags:

The easiest approach to segments such as this is often to copy the source text into the target segment and overwrite the text between the tags with the translation.

The best way to do this is to use the **Copy Source to Target** command.

Copy Source to Target commands

To copy the entire content of the source segment into the target segment, from the **Home** tab, in the **Segments Actions** group or from the right-click menu, choose **Copy Source to Target** (*Ctrl + Insert*), as shown in the following screenshot. You can also find the **Copy Source to Target** button in the toolbar at the top of the **Translation Results** window.

You can use this technique again in **Segment 10** to copy the file hyperlink (which is not recognized as a placeable and translated automatically because it is not a web link beginning with `http://`).

To copy the content of all source segments in the open SDLXLIFF file to their target segments from the **Home** tab, choose **Copy All Source to Target** (*Alt + Shift + Insert*).

 The **Copy Source to Target** command overwrites whatever is already in the target segment, even if the segment has been confirmed or signed off (though not if it has been locked). If you need to restore the overwritten target segment(s), press *Ctrl + Z*. The **Copy All Source to Target** command only affects empty target segments, whatever their status, unless they are locked.

To clear a target segment of all content, from the **Home** tab, in the **Segments Actions** group, choose **Clear Target Segment** (*Alt + Del*).

Removing formatting and tags

To remove all the formatting and tags in a segment, first ensure that, in the **Advanced** tab, the **Protect Tags** option is not selected, as this will prevent you from removing the tags. Click in the target segment and, from the **Home** ribbon, in the **Formatting** group, click the dropdown arrow under the **Clear Formatting** button, and choose **Clear All Formatting**, or press *Ctrl + Alt + Space*. In the sample file, try this in **Segment 11** (use **Copy Source to Target** to copy the text from source to target before you do so).

To remove individual pieces of formatting and/or tags, first select the text (including any tags on either side) and then from the **Home** ribbon in the **Formatting** group, click the **Clear Formatting** button (shown in the following screenshot) or press *Ctrl* + Space.

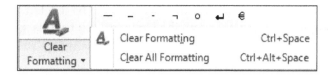

In the sample file, try this in **Segment 12** on the target word for `formatting`.

When using the **Clear Formatting** command to remove formatting such as in **Segment 12**, it is advisable to display and select the tags first, as shown in the following screenshot:

To do this, in the **View** tab, press the **Toggle formatting tag display** button (located in the **Options** group of the ribbon) shown in the following screenshot (or press *Ctrl* + *Shift* + *H*) to display the tags:

Selecting only text without the tags displayed can leave hidden tags in the segment, as shown in the following screenshot (we have toggled the tag display on after removing the formatting for illustration purposes). Hidden tags can always be visualized by clicking **Toggle formatting tag display**.

La mise en forme peut être ennuyante.

Formatting that appears in visual form rather than in tags, such as when you use shortcuts such as *Ctrl* + *B* to apply formatting, is actually controlled using hidden tags and can also be removed in this way.

Ghost tags

Ghost tags are a method of reminding you to keep both halves of a tag pair intact in your target segment. If you delete one half of a tag pair, or fail to insert both halves, the missing half does not disappear, but is displayed in a paler pink color to remind you that it needs to be restored (or the other tag needs to be deleted too). To delete a tag, select it and press the *Delete* key on the keyboard. To try this, go back to **Segment 6** and delete the second tag, as shown here:

To restore the missing tag, select it, and then right-click and choose **Restore Tags** (*Ctrl + Shift + G*) or go to the **Advanced** ribbon and, on the left, click the **Restore Tags** button. Alternatively, press *Ctrl + Z* to undo the delete operation.

Tag verification

By default, SDL Trados Studio will check each segment for tag errors as you confirm it with *Ctrl + Enter*. If you omit (or position incorrectly) tags that affect the functionality of the document, such as hyperlinks and footnotes, you will see a red error notification icon like that in the following screenshot. In most cases, it is not possible to generate the translated document if this happens.

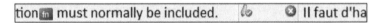

To display information on the reason for the error icon appearing, place your mouse pointer over the red error notification icon in the status column. The following screenshot shows the message in **Segment 13** when the footnote in the source segment has not been added to the target:

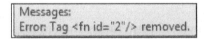

To test this out, omit the footnote tag in **Segment 13**. Confirm the segment and try to generate the target document by choosing **File | Save Target As**. You will get a message saying **Failed to save target content**. Now insert the footnote tag and confirm the segment. The error notification icon will disappear and you will be able to generate the target document.

If SDL Trados Studio does not otherwise allow you to generate the translated document, you may, in some cases, be able to do so using the **Export Files** batch task described in *Chapter 7, Working with Projects*.

By default, omission of tags that represent formatting (as opposed to functionality) does not produce an error. It is up to you to decide whether the formatting is important. To modify the tag verification settings, choose **Project Settings** (to change the settings for the current translation) or **File | Options** (to do so for all subsequent work based on the new global profile setting). Choose **File Types** and select the relevant file type. For example, if this is a .docx file, choose **Microsoft Word 2007-13 | Tag check**. To activate checking of formatting tags, for example, uncheck the option **Ignore formatting tags**.

 For information on the difference between the settings under **Project Settings** and **File | Options**, see *Chapter 7, Working with Projects*.

Summary

In this chapter, you learned about the importance of tags and how to work with them. In the next chapter, we look at how to produce word counts and bill your clients for work done in SDL Trados Studio.

5
Word Counts and Billing Information

In this chapter, we look at how to produce a word count to use in a quotation or invoice. You will learn how to create a report showing the number of matches in various categories and how to use this information for quoting and billing.

About word counts

The process of obtaining statistical information on match levels (that is, the degree of similarity between the content of the available TMs and that of the documents for translation) that you can use to give your client a quotation, create your invoice, or assess for yourself how much time and effort you are likely to have to put into the translation is called analysis. It is done by using the **Analyze Files** batch task to compare the content of the new document(s) for translation to the content of one or more TMs to see how many matches those TMs will produce during translation. Note that the word count in SDL Trados Studio is always based on the source language.

Word counts are given in terms of various match types that can be broadly categorized as:

- **100% matches**: The segment in the document is exactly the same as a segment in the TM.

- **Fuzzy matches**: The segment in the document is similar but not exactly the same as a segment in the TM. The degree of similarity between the segment in the document and the segment in the TM is assigned a percentage that is, by default, between 50% and 99% but can be adjusted to the range desired by the user.

- **New** (or **no match**): The segment in the document has no corresponding segment in the TM with at least the lowest percentage that is configured for fuzzy matches.

Using the sample file

The sample file for this chapter, Chap_05_SampleFile_01.docx, is a modified version of the sample file for *Chapter 3, Translating a File*. For the purpose of this chapter, however, we will not translate it. Instead, we will open it in SDL Trados Studio and perform an analysis against the TM that you used to translate the sample file in *Chapter 3, Translating a File*, (Chap_03_SampleFile_01.docx). This will show you how to obtain a word count by comparing a new document for translation against a TM containing translations that you have done previously. One real-life situation in which this commonly happens is when you receive an updated version of a document that you have translated previously using a TM, and want to **leverage** (that is to say, re-use) that TM to give you matches when you translate the updated document. This is the situation that we are simulating here.

Performing an analysis

This section describes how to analyze an individual document or several files in a project.

Analysis provides a snapshot of the similarity between the document for translation and the TM(s) at that point in time. For invoicing and quoting purposes, it is therefore essential to do the analysis before you start translating. Obviously, if you translate the document and update the TM with its content first and then run the analysis second, the result will be a series of 100% matches, which is no use for quoting or invoicing.

Analyzing an individual document

To analyze an individual document that you have opened in the **Editor** and saved as SDLXLIFF (such as our sample file), perform the following steps:

1. From the **Home** tab, choose **Batch Tasks | Analyze Files**, as shown in the following screenshot (saving the SDLXLIFF first if prompted):

2. In the first screen of the wizard, **Batch Tasks**, click **Next**.

3. The second screen, **Settings**, offers various optional settings. If you are new to the **Analyze Files** task, you may wish to try it with the default settings first. Otherwise, the optional settings and their effects are discussed in a later section, *Configuring the settings*. If you are using the sample file, we suggest that you try running the analysis twice, before and after you configure the settings, and compare the results.

4. Click **Finish** to run the analysis. When the **Performing tasks** window displays the word **Completed**, click **Close** to complete the process.

5. You will now be prompted to reopen the document (because SDL Trados Studio has to close it to perform the analysis). To reopen the document, click **Yes**.

Analyzing files in a project

Using the **New Project** command (from, for example, the middle of the **Welcome** view), you can group several files in one project and then translate and work with some or all of them at once (projects are discussed in detail in *Chapter 7, Working with Projects*).

To analyze all the translation files in a project, go to the **Projects** view. In the list of projects, select the project name. From the **Home** tab or right-click menu, choose **Batch Tasks | Analyze Files** and follow the wizard through as described in the steps in the previous section.

To analyze selected files in a project, go to the **Projects** view. In the list of projects, select the project name. Now go to the **Files** view and select the files you want to analyze. Choose the **Analyze Files** batch task and proceed as described in the steps in the previous section.

Configuring the settings

Changing the **Analyze Files** settings can affect the amount that the translator quotes or bills. This section describes the options for configuring the settings in the **Settings** screen of the **Analyze Files** wizard via the **Analyze Files** and **Fuzzy Bands** areas on the left of the dialog box shown in the following screenshot:

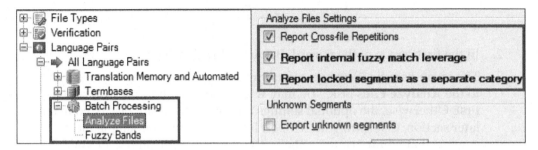

The settings under the **Analyze Files** option are as follows:

- **Report Cross-file Repetitions**: This option (selected by default) is only relevant if you are working with a project containing more than one file for translation. Segments that have no match in the TMs but are duplicates of segments found in other files included in the **Analyze Files** task are reported as a separate category in the **Analyze Files** report. The counts are based on the assumption that you will translate the documents from top to bottom. For example, in a project containing two files, the same segment occurs eight times, three times in File #1 and five times in File #2. The results of the **Analyze Files** report for File #1 are one new segment and two repetitions; and for File #2, five cross-file repetitions.

- **Report internal fuzzy match leverage**: This is a very useful setting when you want to know the number of fuzzy matches that will be generated for segments without a match in the TMs (that is to say "internally", within the documents themselves) when you go through and "translate the document from start to end, segment by segment" (quoted from the SDL help at http://tinyurl.com/internal-fuzzy). When this option is checked, segments that have no match in the TMs but appear in different variations in the documents themselves are counted as fuzzy matches and recorded in the **Analyze Files** report in the **Totals** and **File Details** areas, under a separate **Internal** heading.

For example, if the sentences `Please complete the form now` and `Please complete the form later` appear in the documents but do not produce a match from the TM, the second of these sentences will be recorded as an **internal** fuzzy match. When this option is set, our sample file produces additional fuzzy matches, shown in the screenshot of the **Analyze Files** report later in this chapter in the separate internal fuzzy matches category.

If this option is not checked, fuzzy matches that do not originate from the TM will not be recorded in the **Analyze Files** report (which may therefore not fully reflect the translation effort required).

- **Report locked segments as a separate category**: Segments in SDLXLIFFs can be locked and unlocked by pressing *Ctrl + L* (or from the right-click menu). Locked segments cannot be edited, so project managers can, for example, lock 100% matches if they do not want the translator to change these matches. If this option is selected, locked segments are reported as a separate category at the top of the **Analyze Files** report so that the word count for these segments can be omitted from the word count for translation.

- **Export unknown segments** and **Export frequent segments**: These are project management settings intended for use in large projects when it is desirable to isolate all of the segments that appear in the TMs, respectively, not at all, or more than a specified number of times, as shown in the following screenshot. These segments are placed in an SDLXLIFF file in a subfolder of the project folder, called **Exports**. They can then be translated first to ensure greater consistency once the main translation work begins.

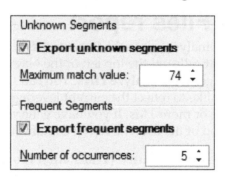

The **Fuzzy Bands** option allows you to change the match ranges reported by default as follows.

By default, fuzzy matches between 50% and 99% are split into four bands, as shown in the screenshot of the **Analyze Files** report in the following section. To adjust the bands that appear in the report, choose **Fuzzy Bands** and then use the arrow keys in the **Min** and **Max** columns to adjust each band up or down, or create and remove bands by selecting the band and pressing the **Split Band** and **Remove Band** buttons at the bottom right.

The following screenshot shows the band settings adjusted for a situation in which we want only fuzzy matches in the range 75% to 99% to be reported in a single band:

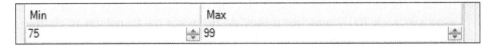

It is not for this book to suggest what arrangements translators should make with their clients. However, it is reasonably safe to say that these default fuzzy bands represent a kind of standard in the translation industry and normally need to be changed only in very specific circumstances. Of course, changing the fuzzy bands will produce different analysis results which, from the perspective of the translator, can be more advantageous (higher word counts and therefore higher pay) or more disadvantageous (lower word counts and therefore lower pay).

The Analyze Files report

To view the results of the analysis, go to the **Reports** view. To open the report (if it does not load automatically), at the top left of the Navigation pane, under the relevant target language, click **Analyze Files**. You can run the **Analyze Files** batch task as often as you like to reflect the current leverage of one or more files for translation against one or more TMs. If you have generated more than one report, the most recent is at the top of the list. The report contains the following elements:

- **Summary**: Includes the TMs used (**Translation Providers**).
- **Settings**: Lists the **Analyze Files** settings described previously, and penalties and other settings in use, which may also affect the results of the analysis.

- **Totals** and **File Details**: The match figures shown in the following screenshot are given for each individual file under **File Details** and as a total for all files analyzed under **Totals**. If you are analyzing more than one file in a project (see *Chapter 7, Working with Projects*), you will be able to see the match figures for each file and for all the files as a total. The following screenshot shows the figures for the sample file against the TM used in *Chapter 3, Translating a File*, with the options to report locked segments and internal fuzzy matches selected.

Total	Type		Segments	Words	Characters	Percent	Recognized	Tokens	Tags
Files:1	Locked		0	0	0	0.00%		0	0
Chars/Word:5.12	PerfectMatch		0	0	0	0.00%		0	0
	Context Match		10	52	308	7.38%		6	0
	Repetitions	100%	7	61	324	8.65%		8	8
	Cross-file Repetitions		0	0	0	0.00%		0	0
	100%		6	44	271	6.24%		3	0
	95% - 99%		1	7	39	0.99%		2	2
	85% - 94%		6	51	301	7.23%		4	0
	75% - 84%	Fuzzy	5	50	263	7.09%		0	0
	50% - 74%	New	0	0	0	0.00%		0	0
	Internal:								
	95% - 99%	Internal	6	53	323	7.52%		2	2
	85% - 94%	fuzzy	7	81	378	11.49%		0	0
	75% - 84%		1	5	27	0.71%		0	0
	50% - 74%	New	0	0	0	0.00%		0	0
	New		23	301	1378	42.70%		3	0
	Total		72	705	3612	100%		28	12

A summary of the **Analyze Files** results is also displayed in the **Files** and **Project** views under the **Analysis Statistics** tab at the bottom of the **SDL Trados Studio** window.

Match types

The following table explains the match types in the report and shows how each is commonly invoiced. Notice that the reliability of the matches increases from bottom to top.

Match type	Description	Usual invoice category
Locked	Segments that have been locked to prevent editing (this category only appears in the report if the option to report locked segments is selected). In the **Editor**, segments can be locked and unlocked by pressing *Ctrl + L* or via the right-click menu.	Omitted
PerfectMatch	Provide more reliability than standard 100% matches by matching against previously translated bilingual documents rather than TMs. For more detail, see *Chapter 7, Working with Projects*.	100% match
Context Match	A more secure version of a 100% match, because the context, as well as the content, of the segment must be the same. Produced when the document segment has the same preceding segment as the segment in the TM had in its original document context, or when both occur at the head of the document. In the sample file, **Segment 1** produces a context match because it is a 100% match that occurs at the head of the sample files in both this chapter and *Chapter 3, Translating a File*. Context matches are indicated by the following icon in the segment status column:	100% match
Repetitions	Reported when a segment not present in the TM occurs more than once in the document. For example, a segment with no match in the TM that occurs 10 times in the document will produce 1 **New** segment (the first instance) and 9 **Repetition** segments (the remaining instances).	100% match
Cross-file Repetitions	Duplicate segments with no match in the TM that occur across different files being analyzed in a project.	100% match
100%	An exact match against a segment in the TM.	100% match
75%-99%	Partial matches usually billed for by translators.	Fuzzy match

Match type	Description	Usual invoice category
50%–74%	Partial matches in this bracket may be counted as fuzzy matches or grouped with the **New** segments.	New or fuzzy match
New	Segments for which there is no match in the TM.	New

Saving the report

It is often convenient to save the report so that you can use it outside SDL Trados Studio. To save the report, from the **Home** tab, or by right-clicking on the report in the Navigation pane, click the **Save As** icon shown in the following screenshot, or press *Ctrl + S*:

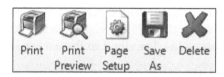

You will be prompted to save the report in one of four formats (.xlsx, .html, .mht, and .xml).

Aggregating the figures

If you are comfortable using Excel, saving the report as .xlsx can be convenient because it allows you to aggregate the figures easily in a separate area of the reports file. The figures can then be copied and pasted from Excel to use in a quotation or invoice.

Often clients do not require all of the detail provided by the **Analyze Files** report. When producing a quotation or invoice, it is common practice to summarize the figures in the **Words** column (or **Characters** column for some Asian languages) of the report into the three categories represented in the earlier screenshot under **Match types** by the red boxes. When aggregated, the figures for the sample file would give the following results (shown here in a table produced in Excel):

	Rate	Words	Amount
100%	$0.06	157	$9.42
Fuzzy	$0.09	247	$22.23
New	$0.12	301	$36.12
Total		705	$67.77

Rates and invoice categories of course depend in reality on what is agreed between the translator and client. The rates shown here are fictitious and offered purely by way of example for the purpose of demonstration.

Analyzing files without a TM

You will sometimes have new documents for translation but no TM that contains matching content. To find out whether the documents themselves contain repeated content, you can analyze them against a dummy (new and empty) TM. In this situation, however, the **Analyze Files** report will, by default, tell you only how many **New** segments and **Repetitions** the documents will generate during translation.

To gauge more accurately the time and effort that the documents will take to translate by checking also how many fuzzy matches the documents will generate, in the **Settings** screen of the **Analyze Files** wizard, select **Analyze Files | Report internal fuzzy match leverage** (as described in the earlier section, *Configuring the settings*).

 Similarly, if you are expecting the TM to produce matches and are surprised that the report shows only **New** matches, **Repetitions**, and **Cross-file repetitions**, it could well be that you have somehow failed to select a TM. To check and modify your TM setup, choose **Home | Project Settings | Language Pairs | All Language Pairs**.

Summary

In this chapter, you learned how to create and interpret reports that allow you to make quotations and invoices. In the next chapter, we look at how to review and edit a translation in SDL Trados Studio.

6
Editing and Quality Assurance

This chapter describes how to make the best of SDL Trados Studio during the review process by introducing you to a number of features designed specifically to help you edit and check your work, such as the **Display Filter**, **Track Changes**, **Comments**, and the **QA Checker**. You will also learn how to work in **Review** mode and to adapt the **Auto-propagate** settings to make them more effective during review.

The sample file for this chapter (`Chap_06_SampleFile_01.docx_en-US_en-GB.sdlxliff`) is an SDLXLIFF that uses a pseudo translation between U.S. and U.K. English (on the basis that most users of the Freelance version will have English as one of their five installed languages and will not therefore be excluded from using the file).

Working in Review mode

SDL Trados Studio has three modes of working, **Translation**, **Review**, and **Sign-off**, which are intended to reflect the stages of the translation process itself, namely translation by a translator, review by a reviewer, and sign-off by a project manager or second reviewer. When you open a file for translation, it opens by default in Translation mode. In practice, many users work only in Translation mode. There is nothing to stop you from working in Translation mode even when you are reviewing or editing a document, but Review mode has certain advantages in this situation.

For example, Review mode has a different screen layout from Translation mode. It is designed to facilitate the review process by giving greater prominence to the side-by-side editor, with the **Comments, Messages,** and **Translation Results** windows at the bottom of the screen. Also, instead of the three Translation-mode segment statuses of **Not Translated, Draft,** and **Translated,** in Review mode the status **Translation Approved** (green tick) and **Translation Rejected** (red cross), shown in the following screenshot, are activated when you confirm or reject segments:

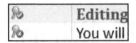

One obvious benefit of working in Review mode is therefore that you can track your progress through the review of the document with the review status icons, as shown in the following screenshot of the progress bar under the side-by-side editor. If, on the other hand, you review your work in Translation mode, the status icons in the progress bar will not differentiate between previously translated segments and those you have reviewed.

The **Confirmation Statistics** tab in the **Files** view also shows the review statuses.

Once assigned to a segment, the review status icons remain in place when the file is closed and reopened in any mode. You can therefore use the review icons to keep tabs on which segments you have reviewed or, by rejecting segments, to indicate those that require attention, such as when returning the SDLXLIFF to the original translator for correction.

Note that **Track Changes** is activated by default in Review mode, so you may wish to turn it on and off depending on whether a particular segment requires it.

Sign-off mode is similar to Review mode in having its own statuses (**Signed off** and **Sign-off Rejected**), but is intended for project managers to indicate their final approval once a document has been reviewed.

Opening a file for review

You cannot open a single file directly for review from the **File** menu. To open a single file for review, first open it with **File | Open | Translate Single Document,** and then save and close it. This automatically generates an SDLXLIFF for the file and takes you back to the **Files** view, where the file is selected in the right-hand pane.

From the **Home** tab, choose the **Open For Review** button (outlined in the following screenshot) or right-click the filename itself and choose **Open For Review**. You can try this now with our sample file (Chap_06_SampleFile_01.docx_en-US_en-GB.sdlxliff).

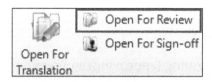

To open a file in a project that you created in the **New Project** wizard for review (see *Chapter 7, Working with Projects*), in the **Projects** view, double-click the name of the project to jump to the **Files** view, select the desired file, and open it for review as described in the preceding paragraph.

The Review tab

When you open a document in the **Editor** view, the **Review** tab appears in the ribbon. The **Review** tab houses many of the main commands that you will be using when you review and edit bilingual documents, and which are described in the rest of this chapter.

Approving and rejecting segments

In Review mode, you have the option of confirming (approving) or rejecting the segments. The **Home** tab contains the following buttons for approving and rejecting segments:

The main actions are as follows:

- To approve a segment, click the **Confirm** button or press *Ctrl + Enter*.
- To reject a segment, click the **Reject Segment** button or press *Ctrl + Shift + Enter*.
- To approve all remaining unreviewed segments in the document in one go, click the **Complete Review** button.

When you exit a document open in Review mode, you will be prompted to decide whether you want to mark all unreviewed segments as approved. To approve all remaining unreviewed segments, click **Yes**. To leave the unreviewed segments in their current state (so that you can come back and review them later, for example), click **No**. This leaves all rejected segments with rejected status (which also makes them easier to work with if you decide next to have a final check made on the document in Sign-off mode).

In the sample file, try confirming (approving) and rejecting **Segments 1 and 2** respectively, then save, close (choosing **No** when promoted to approve all remaining segments), and reopen the SDLXLIFF for review as described in the preceding section.

Moving through a document

When reviewing your work, you can of course move around the SDLXLIFF in the same way as while translating, but the following techniques may also be useful.

- Pressing *Ctrl + Enter* to approve a segment in Review mode moves you to the next segment that is not confirmed as approved or rejected. In the sample file, in **Segment 2**, pressing *Ctrl + Enter* moves you to **Segment 3** (in Translation mode, you would be moved to **Segment 5**). Using *Ctrl + Alt + Enter* approves the current segment, whatever its status, and moves you to the next one down, whatever its status. Using *Ctrl + Shift + Enter* rejects the segment and then moves you to the next one, whatever its status.

- To jump to a particular segment, in the **Home** view, choose **Go To**, or press *Ctrl + G*, and then type the segment number, and press **OK**.

- When you work in the **Editor** view, the area at the top of the Navigation pane will display any heading styles and other structural elements that are present in your source document. Clicking on these elements in the Navigation pane is a quick way to jump straight to the corresponding section in the side-by-side editor, as shown in the following screenshot from the sample file:

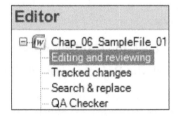

Interpreting the fuzzy match icons

The fuzzy match icons in the segment status column can be useful reviewing aids, reminding you to check whether a fuzzy match has been edited or not. The following screenshot shows **Segments 2, 3, and 4** of the sample file. **Segments 3 and 4** are fuzzy matches generated by **Segment 2** but have different match indicators.

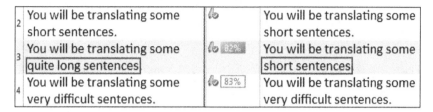

The fuzzy match value in **Segment 3** has a yellow background color. This is because **Segment 3** has been confirmed without the fuzzy match being edited. The words outlined in the box needed changing in the translation, but the translator has omitted to do this and confirmed the segment anyway. In **Segment 4**, the white background on the match indicator **83%** indicates that the segment has been edited before confirming. Note also that you can use the **Display Filter**, introduced later in this chapter, to display only such unedited fuzzy matches.

Checking the spelling

SDL Trados Studio has a built-in spellchecker that works in a similar way to that in MS Word. Misspellings are displayed with a wavy red underline as you type. To correct or ignore a spelling, or add it to the dictionary, right-click on the word in the target segment and choose the relevant option, as shown in the following screenshot from **Segment 5**:

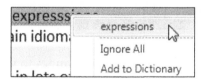

To run a spell-check on a document open in the **Editor**, in the **Review** tab, choose **Check Spelling** (*F7*).

To change the spellchecker options, choose **File | Options | Editor | Spelling**. SDL Trados Studio has two spellcheckers to choose from (MS Word and Hunspell). You can turn interactive spellchecking off by unchecking the box **Check spelling as you type**.

 When you right-click on a word picked up as a misspelling by the spellchecker, the spellchecker menu appears. To display a standard right-click menu, you must first choose to correct or ignore the misspelling and then right-click again.

Working with comments

Comments are useful in two ways: to keep notes for yourself as you translate, and to pass on queries and information about the translation to a reviewer or other person in the workflow. For example, a reviewer can open an SDLXLIFF sent by the translator and view the translator's comments. The reviewer can also respond to the translator's comments in the SDLXLIFF in the form of a comment thread. The main actions that you can perform with comments are as follows:

- **To add a comment to an entire segment**: Click in the segment and, from the **Review** tab or right-click menu, choose **Add Comment** (*Ctrl + Shift + N*). The **Add Comment** dialog box shown in the following screenshot appears. Type the comment and click **OK**.

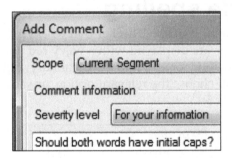

The background color of the segment changes to indicate that a comment has been added (as in the sample file in **Segment 7**, shown in the following screenshot):

Tracked changes

- **To add a comment to a word or string of text inside a segment**: Select the text and, from the **Review** tab or right-click menu, choose **Add Comment** (*Ctrl + Shift + N*). Type the comment and click **OK**. The background color of the selected text changes to indicate that a comment has been added (as in the sample file in **Segment 16**).

- **To add a comment to an entire document**: Click in any segment and, from the **Review** tab or right-click menu, choose **Add Comment** (*Ctrl + Shift + N*). Type your comment. Change the **Scope** option to **Current File**, and click **OK**. A comments symbol appears at the top of the segment status column (as in the sample document), as shown in the following icon:

[For each comment, you can choose a severity level (from **For your information**, **Warning**, and **Error**) to indicate the importance of acting on the comment.]

- **Comments tab**: The **Comments** tab provides an efficient way to work with comments. The tab is located above the side-by-side editor in Translation mode default layout and below it in Review and Sign-off mode default layouts. Click the tab to view a list of comments in the SDLXLIFF. For each comment, the most recently added part of the comment thread is displayed in the list. To display the whole thread in the list, double-click the entry. The first two icons in the following screenshot are to edit or delete the comment selected in the list. The icon on the right is to delete all the comments in the SDLXLIFF.

- **To edit a comment**: Click in the commented text (or, in the case of a comment on the entire document, the icon at the top of the status column). From the **Review** tab or right-click menu, choose **Edit Comment**, then choose **Edit** to edit the existing content of the comment or **Add** to add another comment to the comment (as you would when replying in a thread of messages). Alternatively, select the comment in the **Comments** tab and then click the **Edit Comment** icon at the top of the **Comments** tab. In the sample file, the reviewer has added responses to the comments in **Segments 7 and 16**.

- **To view a comment in the side-by-side editor**: Place your mouse pointer over the text with the colored background in the target segment to display the comment in a tool tip, as shown in the following screenshot of the comment in **Segment 16**:

localization
Comment[Andy, 11/12/2013 16:54:41]: US or UK spelling?

- **To delete a comment**: Click in the commented text and, from the **Review** tab or right-click menu, choose **Edit Comment**, and then **Delete**. Alternatively, use the icons in the **Comments** tab to delete one or all comments.

- **Exporting comments to .docx files**: In the case of .docx files, comments in target segments are, by default, placed in the translated .docx file when the translation is generated (such as via **File | Save Target As**). To change this behavior, the setting that affects it must be changed before the documents for translation are converted to SDLXLIFF format. If you are using the sample file, which is already in an SDLXLIFF format, you will not therefore be able to change this behavior. For an explanation of the reasons for this, see the *Global profile settings versus active project settings* section in *Chapter 7, Working with Projects*.

  To change this setting, before you open the document via **Open Single Document** or create a project that includes the document in the **New Project** wizard, choose **File | Options** and then **File Types | Microsoft Word 2007-2013**. Under **Common**, uncheck the option **Retain Studio target comments in target file**. This change will affect your global profile settings for all future work, unless you reset it later. The **File Types** preferences can also be set up to affect only the current project by changing them in the **New Project** wizard (in the **Project Files** screen) or during an **Open Single Document** operation (in the **Open Document** dialog box, by clicking the **Advanced** button).

- **Extracting comments from .docx files**: You can also decide whether to display comments added in .docx files **As translatable text** or **As Studio comments** in the SDLXLIFF. These options are set under **File Types | Microsoft Word 2007-2013 | Common**, and must be configured before the source files are converted to SDLXLIFF format, as described in the previous paragraph.

Tracking your changes

SDL Trados Studio uses a system for tracking changes that will be familiar to you if you have used the **Track Changes** feature in MS Word and that works in more or less the same way. **Track Changes** is a useful feature for translators reviewing their own work or exchanging information about review changes in the SDLXLIFF with a reviewer.

Activating Track Changes

The **Track Changes** group in the **Review** tab, shown in the following screenshot, has options for toggling **Track Changes** on and off, previewing the effect of tracked changes in the SDLXLIFF, accepting and rejecting changes individually or globally, and moving between tracked changes.

To activate and deactivate **Track Changes**, click the **Track Changes** button, shown on the left in the following screenshot, or press *Ctrl + Alt + F9*. Track Changes is active by default when you open a document in Review or Sign-off mode, but not in Translation mode. This setting can be changed from the **Review** tab, in the Track Changes group, via the options launcher (small arrow icon) at the bottom right, or via **File | Options**.

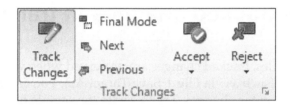

You can use the sample file to try out the techniques described in this section.

Editing your work with Track Changes

The following screenshot of **Segment 8** in the sample file shows a segment containing (in left to right order) a deletion, replacement (addition), and change of formatting, all of which are tracked using colored text:

Tracked Changes ~~are~~is ~~very~~*very* useful in lots of situations.

To display a tool tip showing the name of the reviser and the date and time of the revision, move your mouse pointer over the tracked change.

> Tracked change information cannot be stored in the translation memory. When you confirm a segment containing tracked changes, the memory is updated with the changed version, but the tracked changes remain showing in the SDLXLIFF.

To accept and reject tracked changes, click in the tracked change and choose the appropriate option from the **Track Changes** group. Click the drop-down arrow on the **Accept** and **Reject** buttons to access options for accepting or rejecting changes individually or globally, as shown in the following screenshot:

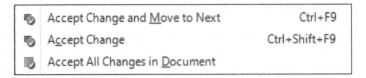

Tracked changes can also be accepted or rejected from the right-click menu.

Preserving tracked changes in translated documents

In the case of .docx files, tracked changes are preserved when you generate the translated document (such as via **File | Save Target As**). You can then use MS Word to accept or reject the changes. Try this with the sample file. For all other file formats (including .doc), the translated document is generated with the tracked changes accepted.

The same applies to .docx and other file formats respectively when using the preview feature under **File | Print & View | View In**.

Previewing the effect of tracked changes

To preview the effect of accepting all of the tracked changes in the **Editor** view, in the **Track Changes** menu, click the **Final Mode** button, shown in the following screenshot:

Click the button again to redisplay the tracked changes.

What if your source file already contains tracked changes?

You can open .docx files containing tracked changes and display the tracked changes in the source column of the **Editor**. If a TM contains a 100% match for the segment as it was prior to the tracked changes, the **TC** icon appears in the Status column and the mouseover displays the information **TM match with source tracked changes rejected**. In the sample file, **Segments 9 and 10** would have been 100% matches for **Segments 4 and 6** were it not for the tracked changes in the source segments. The following screenshot shows how the TC match remains blue (as in **Segment 9**) until the target segment is edited (as in **Segment 10**):

9	You will be translating some ~~very~~ really difficult sentences.
10	There are several sentences that ~~contain~~ include idiomatic expressions.

The **Translation Results** window will also display any matches for the segment with the tracked changes accepted.

Opening a document with tracked changes preserved in the source makes most sense if your TM contains the translation of the source file before the changes were applied. Typically, this arises when you translate an updated version of a file you have already translated using a TM, and the new source document has been updated with Track Changes. Perhaps for this reason, SDL Trados Studio, by default, opens source .docx files containing tracked changes with the changes accepted. To display tracked changes in the source segments in the SDLXLIFF, before you open the .docx file via **Translate Single Document** or create a project that includes it, choose **File | Options | File Types | Microsoft Word 2007-2013 | Common**. Change the **Track changes extraction mode** from **Apply changes before opening** to **Display pending changes**. Click **OK** to exit and then open the file. Note that this will affect your global profile settings for all future work (unless you reset the defaults later).

Find and Replace

The **Find and Replace** feature sits on the right of the **Home** tab in the **Editing** group, and allows you to search for text in the source and target segments, and to replace text in the target segments only.

 The use of **Find and Replace** is limited to files open in the **Editor**. To find and replace text in several SDXLIFFs at a time, use the **SDL Batch Find and Replace** tool or the **QuickMerge** feature, both of which we will discuss in *Chapter 7, Working with Projects*.

The main find and replace actions are as follows:

- **To find text**: Choose **Home | Find** (*Ctrl + F*). In the **Find what** field, type the text, select whether you want to search in the source or the target, and click **Find Next**.

- **To replace text**: Choose **Home | Replace** (*Ctrl + H*). In the **Find what** and **Replace with** fields, type the relevant text and click **Find Next**, followed by **Replace** to replace each instance one by one or **Replace all** to replace all instances in one go. Any changed segments are unconfirmed.

- **Find variations of text**: Wildcards are useful for finding text in different variations to help evaluate the translation of certain text in different contexts. To use wildcards, in the **Find and Replace** dialog box, select **Use** and choose **Wildcards** from the options list. Here are some examples that you can try out in the sample file:
  - The ? character matches a single character at the specified position (including spaces). Thus, `charity?worker` finds **charity worker** and **charity-worker** (but not **charity and other such workers**).
  - The * character matches zero or more characters at the specified position. Thus, `earn * dollars` finds **earn 80,000 dollars** and **earn either 50,000 or 80,000 dollars**.

- **Use regular expressions**: Regular expressions are a powerful means to find and replace text that matches certain patterns. As an example, the sample file contains several digits with measurement units (such as 2 cm). Some have a space between the digit and the unit, while others do not. To correct this inconsistency, we can use regular expressions to find instances with no intervening space and insert the space in all such instances in one operation. This is not possible with a standard find and replace operation, because the digits and numbers are different in each instance.

In the **Find and Replace** dialog box, select **Use** and choose **Regular Expressions** from the options list. In the sample file, searching for `(\d+)(cm|m)` will find one or more digits followed immediately by the letters `cm` or `m` (with no space). To replace each instance found with the digit followed by a space and then the unit, in the **Replace with** field, type `$1 $2`. To learn more about regular expressions, try **The 30 Minute Regex Tutorial** at `http://tinyurl.com/30min-regex`. If you explore this topic further, be aware that SDL Trados Studio uses the .NET flavor of regular expressions.

The Display Filter

The **Display Filter** is a powerful review feature that allows you to limit the display in the Editor to show only segments with certain characteristics. For example, you can display only unconfirmed segments, only segments with comments or tracked changes, or only segments containing certain text strings, so as to isolate difficulties at the review stage and make the task of resolving them more efficient.

The **Display Filter** sits in the **Review** tab, as in the following screenshot:

The main actions in the **Display Filter** are as follows:

- **To display only certain types of segment**: Click the **All segments** dropdown and choose the type of segment to display. For example, choose **With comments** to display only segments with comments so that you can address the issues in the comments from within the document in one go. In the sample file, this will display only **Segments 7, 16, 23, and 29**, and any others to which you have added a comment. Alternatively, filter on **Translation rejected** to show only segments that you have rejected during the review.

- **To redisplay all the segments**: From the dropdown on the left, choose **All segments** and press *Enter*. Alternatively, click the **Reset Filters** button on the right.

- **To display segments containing certain text**: Type the text in the **Search** field, specify whether to filter on the source or target using the dropdown on the left, and press *Enter*. This is a useful way to check how well a particular choice of wording works in different contexts throughout the document. In the sample file, try this with the word **turnover**. The **Display Filter** retains a history of the last things you typed, which will reappear as you type the first letters in the **Search** field.

If you use **Find and Replace** to replace text in the target segments with the **Display Filter** active, only the filtered segments shown in the **Editor** at that time will be changed. This allows you to limit text replacement operations to certain segment contexts. By using the **Display Filter** to display segments containing the words that you want to change before you run the replace operation, you can see in one glance how that change works in all of the affected segments (although by the same token some segments will be hidden, which may prevent you from seeing their surrounding context). As an example, try this in the sample file by using this technique to change all target segment words ending in "ization" to "isation".

It is important to remember that, if you want to replace a certain term throughout the whole SDLXLIFF, you must first reset the **Display Filter** by redisplaying all segments, otherwise you may not catch every instance of the term in the file.

- **To use regular expressions in the display filter**: The **Search** function in the **Display Filter** also works very powerfully with regular expressions. For example, typing **turnover | revenue** will match segments that contain either of the words **turnover** or **revenue** (as in the sample file).

Quality assurance checks

The **QA Checker** in SDL Trados Studio offers a large number of checks that you can pre-automate. The focus is on spotting mistakes that you might otherwise overlook, such as double spaces between words, missing punctuation, and incorrectly inserted numbers. Remember that the **QA Checker** is there to provide an indication of what might potentially be an error. It is up to you to decide whether it actually is or not.

Configuring the QA Checker

To configure the **QA Checker** for the currently active project, from the **Editor**, in the **Home** tab, choose **Project Settings | Verification | QA Checker 3.0**. Alternatively, on the right of the **Review** ribbon, locate the **Quality Assurance** group and click the dialog-box launcher. The majority of the checks are self-explanatory.

In this section, we summarize the main settings, but it is worth experimenting to find the options that work for you.

QA setting	Summary
Segments Verification:	Check for untranslated and empty target segments; segments where the source and target are identical; target segments longer than the source by a specified percentage; forbidden characters (characters that you specify must not occur in the translation, such as obsolete kanji in Japanese).
Segments to Exclude:	Exclude certain segments from the check based on the segment status and other criteria to reduce the number of mistakes reported unnecessarily.
Inconsistencies:	Check for inconsistent translations (more than one translation for the same segment); repeated words in the target (such as "the the"); unedited fuzzy matches.
Punctuation:	Check for consistency of ending punctuation between source and target; correct use of Spanish punctuation; spaces before punctuation (with a French-compliant option); multiple spaces; multiple dots; extra spaces at the end of the target (which will produce an extra space between consecutive sentences in paragraphs in the translated file); consistency of opening capitalization; global capitalization (if the source segment is entirely in capitals, that the target is also); that brackets consist of an opening and closing bracket pair.
Numbers:	Check that numbers, times, dates, and measurements in the target are the same as in the source segment.
Word List:	Configure incorrect and correct forms of text strings (for example, specify that incorrect form = **Co Ltd**, correct form = **Co., Ltd.**). Once added to the **Word List**, incorrect forms can be quickly and conveniently replaced with their correct form during the correction process. To add an entry to the **Word List**, click the **Check word list** option, enter the incorrect and correct forms, and from the **Action** list, choose **Add Item**.
Regular Expressions:	Build your own customized checks using regular expressions.
Trademark Check:	Check that various trademark characters and symbols are correctly included in the target segment (to add characters to the list, proceed as described previously under **Word List**).

QA setting	Summary
Length Verification:	Check for target segments longer than file-specific limits or a specified number of characters (useful when translating screen text in localization projects and so on).
QA Checker profiles:	Once configured, your settings can be saved for later re-use by clicking **Export settings**. To re-use previously saved settings, click **Import settings**. This way, you can define and use different QA settings for different clients or projects.

To test the **QA Checker** out, we will run some checks on the deliberate errors in our sample file. For example, set up the following checks:

1. Under **Segments Verification**, uncheck the box **Check for forgotten and empty translations**. Our sample file contains some empty segments, but in this case we do not want them to be reported as errors.

2. Under **Inconsistencies**, activate the option **Check for repeated words in target**.

3. Under **Punctuation**, activate the options **Check for multiple spaces** and **Check for multiple dots** and **Check for extra space at end of target segment**.

Notice that the severity level can be set separately for each option (in order of increasing severity, **Note**, **Warning**, or **Error**, shown together in the following screenshot), so that you can decide for yourself how important each type of reported mistake will be:

Under **Word List**, click **Check word list**. For the wrong and correct forms, type **DOLLARS** and **dollars** respectively, and then choose **Action | Add item** to add the check to the list. Change the severity level at the top-right of the **Word List** window from **Warning** to **Error**.

Verifying a file

Once configured, the **QA Checker** will check each segment as you confirm it (with the exception under **Inconsistencies** of the option **Check for inconsistent translations**, which only works when you run a QA check on the entire document). Potential mistakes are represented by an icon in the segment status column corresponding to the severity level assigned to that category of mistake.

To check the entire document open in the **Editor**, choose **Review** | **Verify** (*F8*) or click the **Verify** button shown in the following screenshot. If you are using the sample file and have set up the checks described in the preceding section, do this now.

To check all of the files in a project (see *Chapter 7, Working with Projects*), go to the **Projects** view. Select the project in the projects list and, from the **Home** tab or right-click menu, choose **Batch Tasks** | **Verify Files**, and follow the wizard.

> When you run **Verify Files** as a batch task, any settings already configured for your project will be applied, but you can if necessary modify them in the final screen of the wizard, **Settings**, by choosing **Verification** | **QA Checker 3.0**.

To turn the **QA Checker** off (so that each segment does not get checked as you confirm it), choose **Project Settings** | **Verification**. On the right, uncheck **QA Checker 3.0**.

Keeping a record of mistakes reported

When you verify a document open in the **Editor** as described in the previous section, potential mistakes are listed in the **Messages** window above the side-by-side editor. However, you can also produce a **Verify Files** report to record the mistakes reported by the **QA Checker**. To produce the report when your document is open in the **Editor** view, perform the following steps:

1. In the **Home** tab, choose **Batch Tasks** | **Verify Files** and follow the wizard through to completion.

2. Go to the **Reports** view, where you will see a **Verify Files** report (the most recent report is at the top of the list). The report shows the number of mistakes reported and displays them in a list, as shown in the following screenshot:

	Chap 06 SampleFile 01.docx en-US en-GB.sdlxliff
Information	Extra blank spaces detected.
ⓘ Warning	Target segment contains extra space at the end.

Click in the filename hyperlink to jump to the file so that you can review and correct the mistakes. To save the report in another format, such as Excel, in the **Home** tab, click the **Save As** button or press *Ctrl + S*.

> To produce a **Verify Files** report on all the files in a project (see *Chapter 7, Working with Projects*), go to the **Projects** view, select the project in the list, and from the **Home** tab or right-click menu, choose **Batch Tasks | Verify Files**, and then follow the wizard.

Correcting reported mistakes

Once you have run the QA check, the reported mistakes will be listed along with any tag verification issues in the **Messages** tab (above the side-by-side editor in Translation mode default layout but below it in Review or Sign-off default layout), as shown in the following screenshot:

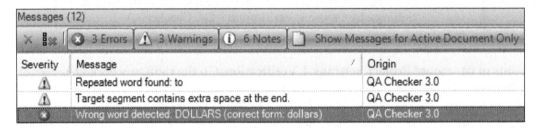

> If you cannot see the **Messages** window, you can open it from the **View** menu, in the **Information** group, from where you can also open the **Concordance Search** and other windows.

To correct the mistakes, double-click on a segment in the **Messages** window. This displays the **Verification Message Details** dialog box (shown in the following screenshot), which can be used to correct mistakes quickly and conveniently. When correcting errors in this way, ensure that **Track Changes** is deactivated first, as it can interfere with the correction process:

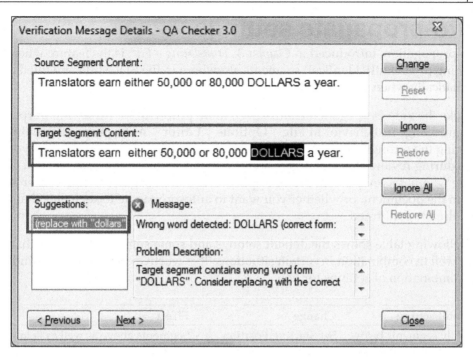

Some mistakes, such as extra spaces, repeated words, or entries in the word list, can be rectified at the click of a button. In such cases, the **Suggestions** field will show the proposed replace action. To make the correction, click **Change**. The next mistake is then displayed.

Other mistakes, such as when the source and target are identical, require an intervention from the translator. Even so, there is no need to go back to the segment in the **Editor** to make the change. The mistake can be corrected by typing directly in the **Target Segment Content** field highlighted in the screenshot. Make the correction and click **Change**.

The fault notification icons in the segment status column disappear when you correct a mistake. If you click **Ignore**, the fault notification icons remain in the segment status column and the mistake is grayed out in the **Messages** window.

Auto-propagate settings

Auto-propagation, introduced in *Chapter 3, Translating a File*, is the feature whereby matching (by default, identical) segments elsewhere in the SDLXLIFF are filled out automatically when you confirm a segment.

To make the auto-propagation feature even more powerful for reviewing purposes, you can change its behavior in **File | Options | Editor | Auto-propagation**. By changing the settings, you can control more effectively how the changes that you make during review affect other segments in the SDLXLIFF. For example, you can decide whether a revision should be applied to identical segments both earlier and later in the document, or whether you want to auto-propagate to segments that you have already confirmed.

The following table shows the default settings and some suggested changes that work well in combination in certain situations. It is worth experimenting to find the best combination of settings for you.

Default setting	Change	Effect
1) Only segments below the current segment are auto-propagated, and not those above	Set **Starting Position** to **First segment in document**	Segments above as well as below are auto-propagated. If you edit and confirm a segment, all 100% matching segments in the SDLXLIFF are updated.
2) Already confirmed segments are not auto-propagated	Check the option **Auto-propagate exact matches to confirmed segments**	Even if a segment has already been confirmed, it is updated when changes are made to a 100% match elsewhere in the bilingual file.
3) Auto-propagated segments remain unconfirmed (even previously confirmed segments are unconfirmed when auto-propagated)	Check the option **Confirm segment after auto-propagating an exact match**	Set this option if you do not want to have to check and reconfirm such segments. This works well in combination with option 2, because you may well edit the same segment translation more than once during a review.
4) Matches are always auto-propagated (based on the other auto-propagation settings) without the user being prompted	Under **Prompt User**, choose **Conditionally when:** and **Matching segment has been translated differently**	If the document contains a different translation for the same source segment, you are prompted to keep or replace the alternative translation when the segment is auto-propagated.

The following screenshots (with segment numbers added on the left) show these settings in action. In each case, the first of the three segments has already been confirmed, thereby auto-propagating the second and third instances of the segment further down the SDLXLIFF, as shown in the following screenshot of **Segments 31 to 33** in the sample file.

To simulate these examples in the sample file, first confirm the segment in each group of three, and then configure the settings for each example. Finally, revise and confirm the middle segment of the three to see the effects described in the examples. For our demonstration, we have worked in Translation mode. If you are working in Review mode, deactivate **Track Changes** before you go through these examples in the sample file.

31		This is a dialog box.
32	100%	This is a dialog box.
33	100%	This is a dialog box.

Example 1: In the situation shown in the following screenshot of **Segments 31 to 33**, the default settings are used. The middle segment is changed to a different translation and confirmed, thereby auto-propagating the last segment below, but not the first segment above. The auto-propagated last segment is left unconfirmed.

31		This is a dialog box.
32	100%	This is a dialogue box.
33	100%	This is a dialogue box.

Example 2: In the situation in the following screenshot of **Segments 35 to 37**, settings 1, 2, and 3 from the preceding table are used. The middle segment is changed to a different translation and confirmed. This time both the last segment, below, and the first segment, above, are auto-propagated.

35	100%	Working with screenshots
36	100%	Working with screenshots
37	100%	Working with screenshots

Setting 2 ensures that the first and last segments, which were already confirmed with different translations to the middle one, are auto-propagated with the revised translation. Setting 3 ensures that the first and last segments are both left confirmed after auto-propagation.

Example 3: In the situation in the following screenshot of **Segments 39 to 41**, setting 4 is used together with settings 1, 2, and 3:

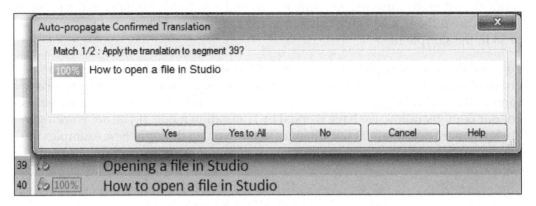

When **Segment 40** is changed to a different translation and confirmed, we are prompted to decide whether or not to auto-propagate the revised translation to every identical segment that currently has a different translation to **Segment 40**, such as **Segment 39** immediately above this segment.

Auto-propagation can be turned off by unchecking the **Enable Auto-propagation** option.

Segments with tracked changes are not auto-propagated until the changes are accepted or rejected, regardless of the auto-propagation settings. It is therefore often worth running an inconsistency check via the **QA Checker** after revising the document. This averts the risk of leaving repeated segments unchanged when the segment producing the auto-propagation has changed.

[Auto-propagation is a feature of the SDLXLIFF file and does not depend on the TM. Auto-propagation therefore works even if you do not have a TM enabled.]

Converting SDLXLIFFs to Word documents

If you need to send bilingual documents for review to a person who does not have access to SDL Trados Studio, you can (regardless of the original document format from which the SDLXLIFFs were produced) convert SDLXLIFFs to a two-column, bilingual **docx review document** that includes comments and tracked changes from the SDLXLIFF.

You can then reimport the reviewed documents to update the SDLXLIFFs with the reviewer's changes, including comments and tracked changes made in the Word review document. Note that the reviewer must use .docx format, or the reimport will not work.

To create a review document for a completed translation, in the **Projects** view, right-click the project, choose **Batch Tasks | Export for External Review**, and follow the wizard. In the final screen (**Settings**), the **Location** field includes a customizable location, which is, by default, set to be a subfolder of the project folder named **External Review**, and which you are prompted to open when you complete the wizard. You can also change the **Layout type** between **Side-by-side** and **Top-down**. The following screenshot shows a side-by-side review document in Word with a tracked changed and a comment made in SDL Trados Studio. The **Segment ID** and **Segment status** are indicated on the left:

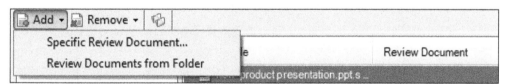

Segment ID	Segment status	Source segment	Target segment		
1	Draft (CM)	Application Fees	Droits d'inscription		
2	Draft (CM)	Administration Fees	Cotisations		Comment [A1]: Is this the correct term?
3	Translated (0%)	Bank Interest	Intérêts bancaires		

To reimport modified review documents, choose **Batch Tasks | Update from External Review**, and follow the wizard. In the **Update from an External Review Document** screen, to pair the project files with their respective review documents, choose **Add** and then **Specific Review Document** or **Review Documents from Folder**, as shown in the following screenshot. Click **Finish** to complete the reimport process.

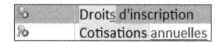

In the **Editor**, modified segments in the SDLXLIFF have (by default) **Translation Rejected** status, and any updated comments and tracked changes are reflected, as in the following screenshot:

Droits d'inscription
Cotisations annuelles

Note that only changes in the target column are reimported to the SDLXLIFF. Formatting changes in the .docx review file are not reflected in the SDLXLIFF. If a target segment has been left empty before export, translations entered in the .docx review file do not appear in the SDLXLIFF after update.

Summary

In this chapter, you have learned various techniques to make editing and reviewing a piece of translation work more efficient. In the next chapter, we look at the advantages of working with the **New Project** feature to create a project, which include the ability to process and translate a number of files as part of the same group and more easily to store and re-use your translation settings.

7
Working with Projects

In earlier chapters, you learned how to open an individual document for translation. What if you want to translate a set of multiple files as part of the same job? This chapter explains how to work with a group of files by creating a project using the **New Project** feature. Projects also have other advantages discussed in this chapter, such as storing and reusing translation settings, and so they are often used to translate single files as well. We finish by introducing a number of tools for project managers, including project packages, which are a handy way to share material with another person in the translation workflow.

Working in a project

As you learned in *Chapter 3, Translating a File*, when you translate a single file with the **Translate Single Document** approach and first save the file, thereby creating the SDLXLIFF, SDL Trados Studio automatically creates a project file (with the extension .sdlproj). However, you can also create your own projects to house one or more files for translation. A project acts as a container for the following:

- All the files that you are translating or using for reference (which we will refer to collectively as project files)
- Any TMs, termbases, and AutoSuggest dictionaries that you use
- Any settings that you configure in SDL Trados Studio

This applies irrespective of whether you are translating a single file or several files (except that a single file project cannot contain reference files).

Reasons to use a project

Using the **New Project** feature to create a project has a number of advantages, some of which are as follows:

- Projects are a convenient way of translating a group of files as part of the same job. The translation or review part of the process for each file is exactly the same as with the **Translate Single Document** approach. Projects, however, provide a more intuitive way to benefit from matching content across more than one file.

- Projects also offer more powerful options in terms of running tasks on several files all at once rather than on each separate file. For example, you can run an analysis or generate the translated documents for all the project files together instead of repeating the task for each one individually.

- Projects allow you to store the settings that you use during translation, and review and re-use them later. For example, if you always use certain TMs, termbases, and specific QA Checker settings for a particular client, when you receive new work from that client, you can use a previous project, or a project template, as the basis to create a new project that will pick up all of those settings automatically.

- Projects can contain several target languages, and provide a neat way for project managers to manage the SDLXLIFFs for each target language and distribute them to different translators.

Creating a project

In this section, we will describe how to create a project, focusing on the main settings to look out for in each screen of the **New Project** wizard. The following example assumes that you are translating several files into one target language, and that the project settings will be configured from scratch, rather than reusing those from a previous project.

In creating the project, SDL Trados Studio automatically makes a copy of your source files in the project folder (in the source languages sub-folder named, for example, en-US). The original source files are left in their original location, and once selected in the **New Project** wizard described in this section, not used again by the project. This means that you do not have to make a new copy of your source files especially to use for the project. Instead, you can just add them from their existing location during the steps described in this section.

To create a project, perform the following steps:

1. In the **Projects** view, from the **Home** tab (or from the **Welcome** screen), click the **New Project** button (*Ctrl + N*), shown in the following screenshot:

2. In the **Project Type** screen, leave the option **Create a project based on a project template** as **Default** (for the other options in this screen, see the section titled *Reusing your project settings* later in this chapter on how to re-use settings from previous projects).

3. In the **Project Details** screen, specify the **Project Name** (this is the name by which the project will appear in the list of projects in the **Projects** view, so make sure that it identifies your project clearly), and then choose the **Location**. This must be an *empty* folder (which we refer to in the rest of this chapter as the **project folder**), so create a new one at this point if necessary.

   Description, Due Date, and **Customer** are optional settings that will appear in the **Projects** view to provide additional information about the project. They are most likely to be useful if you work with many projects simultaneously.

   The option **Allow source editing for supported file types** will allow you to make changes to the source segments during translation (in .doc (MS Word 2000-2003), .docx, .ppt (Microsoft PowerPoint XP-2003), and .pptx files only). It can also be activated by going to **Project Settings | Project** after project creation.

4. In the **Project Languages** screen, select the source and target languages. A project has only one source language, but can be given multiple target languages. SDL Trados Studio will create a separate folder for each target language in the project folder, in which the translations will eventually be placed (in SDLXLIFF and, when generated, the original document format).

5. In the **Project Files** screen, there are three options for adding project files (that is, the files for translation as well as any reference files, if applicable), shown in the next screenshot of the **Project Files** screen.

   ° To add the project files in the same folder without specifying a folder structure, click **Add Files**, select the files in their folder, and click **OK**.

- ° To add the project files in their existing folder structure (including subfolders), select the folder, and click **Add Folder**.
- ° To create a new folder structure within the existing project folder to which to add project files, click **New Folder**.

To remove files or folders, right-click them and choose **Remove**. Note that this will only remove files or folders from within SDL Trados Studio; you are not deleting the actual files or folders on your computer.

The following screenshot shows a situation where the project files have been added in an existing folder structure. Click the folder icons on the left to display on the right the files that they contain.

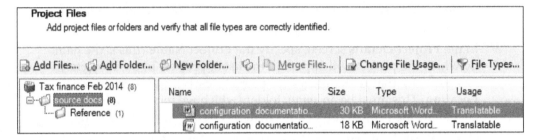

Project files added in a folder structure are displayed with this folder structure in the **Files** view, as in the preceding screenshot (and the folder structure is also retained in the target language folders). This can be useful when you want to perform an operation on certain project files only, by allowing you to isolate those files easily. For example, you can right-click the files in a particular folder in the **Files** view to run batch tasks such as **Analyze Files** on those files only. This method is also useful if you need to retain a certain folder structure, such as when you are translating a website.

For information about file usage, see the section titled *About file usage* later in this chapter.

6. In the **Translation Memory and Automated Translation** screen, under **All Language Pairs**, add existing or create new TMs. If you have more than one target language, do this for each. **Penalties** and other TM settings can also be configured here. To add an AutoSuggest Dictionary, select the relevant language pair on the left and choose **AutoSuggest Dictionaries**.

7. In the **Termbases** screen, click **Add** to add the desired termbases. Using a termbase is optional and you can skip this screen if you do not have or do not want to use a termbase.

8. In the **SDL PerfectMatch** screen (this feature is available only in the Professional version of Studio; you will not see it if you are using the Freelance version), click **Next** to ignore this screen, or under **Previous Document**, select any previously translated SDLXLIFF or TTX files to pair with your project files (the **PerfectMatch** topic is addressed in more detail later in this chapter).

9. The **Project Preparation** screen lists the tasks that SDL Trados Studio will now perform on your project files to finish creating the project. The usual choice here is to leave the **Task Sequence** as **Prepare without project TM** (as an alternative, the **Prepare** task is used to create a project with project TMs, a concept described later in this chapter. Project TMs can be very useful in project management situations). The tasks listed in the **Batch tasks** list tell you that SDL Trados Studio will create SDLXLIFFs from your project files, make a copy of your project files in the project folder, and run certain batch tasks on them such as **Analyze Files** and **Pre-translate files**.

10. The **Batch Processing Settings** screen allows you to modify the **Analyze Files** and **Pre-translate files** settings. The corresponding reports will be available in the **Reports** tab once the project is created.

11. In the **Project Summary** screen, click **Finish**.

12. Wait until the **Preparing Project** screen shows that all tasks have **Completed**. The **Project Template** options are now displayed at the bottom of the screen. To save your project settings for subsequent re-use, choose **Create a new project template based on this project** and then click **Close** and save your project template file. Alternatively, to exit the wizard without saving the project settings, leave the default setting and click **Close**.

 To create a project template from an existing project in the projects list, from the **Home** view or the right-click menu, choose **Create Project Template**.

About file usage

Any file in a format that is translatable in SDL Trados Studio is, by default, assigned the **Usage** of **Translatable**, as you can see on the right of the preceding screenshot. Translatable files are converted to SDLXLIFF format and included in the **Analyze Files** and **Pre-translate files** word counts when the project is created.

To specify that a file is not for translation but to be used for reference, select or right-click the file and choose **Change File Usage | Reference**. Reference files are excluded from the word counts and do not get converted to SDLXLIFF format. If you double-click them in the **Files** view, they will open in their native format instead of in the Editor.

The **Localizable** usage is for designating project files that need translating but cannot be translated in SDL Trados Studio (usually these are image files with embedded text that has to be dealt with in an image editor). No word counts or SDLXLIFFs are produced for such files.

> You might find that MS Word files intended for translation are occasionally and against expectation given the usage **Reference** instead. If this happens, and you cannot change the usage to **Translatable**, try saving the files in a different format (from .doc to .docx or .rtf, for example) and reselecting them.

Translating files in a project

This section describes how to work with a project once you have created it. Any projects that you create are added to the projects list in the **Projects** view, with, as default, the most recently added project at the top, as shown in the following screenshot:

Name	Status	Date Due
Chapter 7 demo project	In Progress	30/01/2014 18:00:00
Accounts En-Fr Jan 2014	In Progress	[none]
Sample Project	In Progress	[none]

One of the most useful features of projects is that they stay in the **Projects** view when you shut down and reopen SDL Trados Studio. In other words, you do not have to go through the process of locating the project files on your hard drive each time you want to resume work on them. Instead, you can simply access them from the **Projects** view. This applies equally to documents translated with the **Translate Single Document** method.

- To open a project file for translation or review, double-click the project in the **Projects** view. This takes you straight to the **Files** view, which displays the individual files in the project, as shown in the following screenshot. The **Progress** indicator on the right updates as you translate each file.

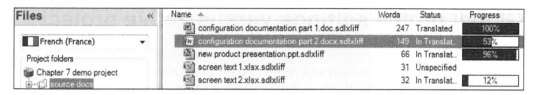

- To display the files in a folder structure, click the folder icon on the left.
- To open a file in Translation mode, double-click the file. Alternatively, select the file in the list and choose the mode in which you want to open it (Review mode, for example) from the **Home** tab in the **Open** group, or right-click to access the same options.

Opening an existing project

To open a project not displayed in the **Projects** view, choose **File | Open Project** (*Ctrl + O*). In the project folder, select the blue project file (.sdlproj), shown here:

The project will now appear in the **Projects** view. To open an entire project on a different machine from the one on which it was created, copy the project folder (along with any TMs and other resources used by the project) over first. If you do this, ensure that the folder structures on the source and target machines are identical. For example, if the TM is stored in D:\TMs and the project in Z:\Projects, the target machine must have access to both folders on the same drives and with the same relative folder structure; otherwise, SDL Trados Studio may be unable to locate the TMs and other resources.

Global profile settings versus active project settings

Understanding the way translation settings and other user preferences are applied is essential for working effectively with SDL Trados Studio. You will find the options for configuring your translation settings in two places: **File | Options**, and **Project Settings** (which appears in the **Home** tab in each view). Both are shown in the following screenshot:

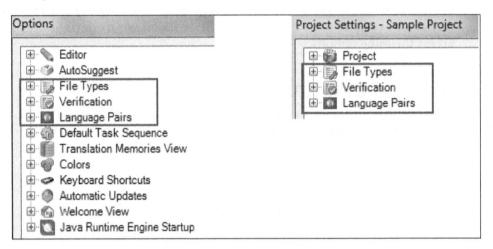

Three of the settings groups appear in both, namely **File Types**, **Verification**, and **Language Pairs**. For these duplicated settings groups, which are outlined in the preceding screenshot, the key points to remember are as follows:

- The three duplicated settings groups in **File | Options** define how SDL Trados Studio will behave the next time you create a new project or open a new document for translation. Changes to these settings will not affect files currently open in the **Editor** or projects that you have already created. We will refer to them as the global profile settings.

- The settings under **Project Settings**, on the other hand, are used to affect the behavior only of specific projects to which you apply them, that is to say, by changing the settings for projects that you have already created in the **New Project** wizard or documents currently opened via **Translate Single Document**. We will refer to them as the active project settings. These settings are also available when you open a file via **Translate Single Document**; to access them, in the **Open Document** dialog box, click the **Advanced** button. In the **New Project** wizard, they can be found at the end of the wizard, in the **Project Summary** screen, via the **Project Settings** button at the bottom right.

- For these duplicated options, the active project settings (set via **Project Settings**) always overrule the corresponding global profile settings (set via **File** | **Options**).

- If you have made changes to the default settings of a particular settings group under **File** | **Options**, you can restore them to default by selecting the relevant settings group on the left of the **Options** window and clicking the **Reset to Defaults** button at the bottom left.

The remaining groups under **File** | **Options** affect both the active project and future behavior. These groups generally contain settings less likely to be specific to any one translation or project, such as font sizes, spellchecker options, or default keyboard shortcuts. You can therefore use them to configure your own standard settings for all work that you do in SDL Trados Studio from that point forward. The remaining group under **Project Settings** is **Project**, which houses basic settings about the active project (such as its name and location).

The following table illustrates the different uses of the global profile and active project settings for the options under **File Types**, **Verification**, and **Language Pairs**:

	Use of File	Options	Use of Project Settings
Verification	To set up or modify the **Verification** options (including **QA Checker**) with new default settings to run on all files that you open via **Translate Single Document** or include in a project created in the **New Project** wizard from this point forward.	To set up or modify the **Verification** options to run on a file currently opened in the Editor (via **Translate Single Document**) or included in a project that you have created in the **New Project** wizard. These settings will override the settings in **File**	**Options**.
Language Pairs	To set up the TMs and other resources used in all future projects, such as by adding or removing TMs, termbases, or AutoSuggest Dictionaries, changing the TM settings (for example, penalties or minimum match value), or configuring default preferences for Batch Tasks such as **Analyze Files**.	To reconfigure the TMs and other resources and settings described in the **Use of File**	**Options** column in a way particular to the active project only (such as if you decide that you want to use an additional TM on a document that you have started translating in the **Editor**). These settings will override the settings in **File**	**Options**.

	Use of File | Options	Use of Project Settings
File Types	**File Types** are the means by which SDL Trados Studio extracts text in different types of document for translation. Some examples are: for MS Word, you can specify whether you want comments to be made available for translation in the **Editor**; for PowerPoint, you can specify whether or not presenter notes are to be included for translation; for Excel, you can specify whether or not worksheet names are to be extracted for translation. Changes to **File Types** are, by their nature, likely to be project- or project template-specific. If you have made changes to these settings under **File | Options** that you do not want to be permanent, you may wish to restore the original default settings before your next project.	**File Types** settings generally take effect at the point when the source document is converted to bilingual format (such as on being opened in the **Editor** via **Translate Single Document** or processed in the **New Project** wizard). They have no effect after this stage, that is to say on SDLXLIFFs that have already been created (whether as part of a multi-file project or by saving a single document in the Editor). To configure **File Types** for a particular project, change the settings during the **New Project** wizard (in the **Project Files** screen) or when using **Open Single Document** (in the **Open Document** dialog box, by clicking the **Advanced** button).

Tuomas Kostiainen has written a useful blog article on this topic, which will allow you to explore it in more depth. See `http://tinyurl.com/trados-settings`.

In practice, an efficient way to control changes to your translation settings is to create project templates, dealt with in the following section, *Reusing your project settings*.

Reusing your project settings

The reusable content in a project includes the selected languages, TMs, termbases, and AutoSuggest Dictionaries, as well as — importantly — any batch-processing settings that you have configured (such as **QA Checker** or **Analyze Files**). If you use a similar setup from one project to the next, you can therefore save time by reusing your settings.

To re-use the settings stored in a project template file created at the end of the project-creation process described earlier in this chapter, do as follows.

In the first screen of the **New Project** wizard, under **Create a project based on a project template**, select a project template from the drop-down list, or browse to select it from a folder. Alternatively, select **Create a project based on a previous project** and select a project from the drop-down list or browse to find the .sdlproj file for the desired project.

When you create a new project from a project template, the settings from the project template are configured automatically during project creation. You can tweak them (such as by adding new TMs or **Analyze Files** settings) as necessary each time you re-use the template. When you go through the **New Project** wizard, you can therefore leave most of the settings unchanged, except:

- In the **Project Details** screen, set the name and location for the new project
- In the **Project Files** screen, add the new file(s) for translation

Useful options in the Projects view

By default, projects listed in the **Projects** view have the status **In Progress**. If you work with lots of projects and want to distinguish those that you have completed, you can change a project's status to **Completed** by right-clicking and choosing **Mark as Complete**. To change the status back to **In Progress**, right-click and choose **Revert to In Progress**.

To remove a project from the list, right-click and choose **Remove from List** (*Ctrl + Alt + F4*). This does not delete the project from your computer; it can be reopened by choosing **File | Open | Open Project**.

Adding files to an existing project

To add project files to an existing project, double-click the project in the **Projects** view to jump to the **Files** view. At the top of the Navigation pane, click in the languages dropdown and select the source language of the project.

To modify the folder structure or change the usage of the project files, in the Navigation pane, select the project or folder name and right-click or, in the **Home** tab, choose the desired action from the **File Actions** group, shown in the following screenshot:

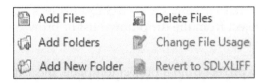

To add the new project files, choose **Add files** and browse to select the files. Alternatively, you can drag-and-drop files into the **Files** view. Once the new project files appear in the files list, select them and, from the **Home** tab or right-click menu, choose **Batch Tasks**. The **Batch Tasks** menu now displays the same tasks that you saw earlier in the **Project Preparation** screen when you first created the project. To ensure that the new project files are processed in the same way as the existing ones, choose the same task as when you created the project (usually **Prepare without project TM**) and follow the instructions in the wizard.

This creates the SDLXLIFFs ready for translation and adds a new **Analyze Files** report to the **Reports** tab covering only the newly processed project files.

Finally, to make the new project files available to open in the **Editor**, reselect the target language in the Navigation pane.

Generating and locating translated documents

This section describes how to generate original file format versions of all your project files in one go (usually after you have translated them in the **Editor**). We also show you how to find them in the project folder or export them to a folder of your choice so that you can, for example, send them to your client.

You can use the following approaches to generate the translated versions of your project files:

- **Generate Target Translations**: Close any SDLXLIFFs that are still open in the **Editor**. Switch to the **Projects** view, and select the project. From the **Home** tab or right-click menu, choose **Batch Tasks | Generate Target Translations**, and then complete the wizard.

This places copies of the (translated) original format documents in a subfolder of the project folder named for the target language (such as `fr-FR` or `de-DE`). To access the project folder from the **Projects** view, select the project and, from the **Home** tab or right-click menu, choose **Open Project Folder** (*Ctrl + Alt + O*). Alternatively, in the **Files** view, right-click on the name of a file in the project and choose **Explore Containing Folder**. You can also navigate to the respective folder using Windows Explorer.

- **Export Files**: SDL Trados Studio provides an easy way for you to copy the translated documents to a convenient folder of your choice without having to look for them in the project folder. In the Projects view, select the project name and choose **Batch Tasks | Export Files**. In the **Settings** screen, under **Batch Processing | Export Files**, specify the export location (as shown in the following screenshot), and then click **Finish**:

To export your files as SDLXLIFFs instead (for sending to a reviewer, for example), change **File version to export** to **Latest bilingual version**.

> Once you have applied the **Generate Target Translations** batch task, most of the options in the **Batch Tasks** menu disappear, because SDL Trados Studio assumes that you are no longer translating the files. To restore the options to the **Batch Tasks** menu, in the **Files** view, select the project files and, from the **Home** tab or right-click menu, choose **Revert to SDLXLIFF** (this can also be done on several selected files at once).

Useful batch tasks

Batch tasks can be run at any time on an entire project, selection of one or more project files, or individual files opened via **Translate Single Document** (provided the individual file has been saved as SDLXLIFF first). To run a batch task on a project, in the **Projects** view, select the project and, from the **Home** tab or right-click menu, choose **Batch Tasks**. To run a batch task on one or more individual files, in the **Files** view, select the file(s) and choose **Batch Tasks**.

The following are some of the most commonly used of these batch tasks:

- **Update Main Translation Memories**: Any TMs that are enabled and set to update are updated with the translations in the SDLXLIFFs based on the segment statuses (such as **Translated** and **Translation Approved**) that you specify. Project managers often use this technique at the end of a project to ensure that the translation memories contain the final, approved versions of the translations. For example, if you add a new TM to a project and want to update it with the content of the project files, this is the way to do it.

- **Finalize**: A handy way to generate all of your translated documents and ensure that your translation memories are up-to-date in a single operation. **Finalize** consists of **Update Main Translation Memories** and **Generate Target Translations**.

- **Pre-translate Files**: This option populates the target segments of the project files with content from the selected translation memories. By default, project files are pre-translated when you create the project, but you may want to apply the content of other TMs that you add to the project later, for example. The **Settings** screen of the **Pre-translate Files** wizard allows you to specify which TMs to pre-translate from, choose a match level to apply, and specify via the **Translation overwrite mode** option which segments get overwritten or retained. There are useful options for confirming and/or locking 100% and context matches, and for copying source to target in segments for which no TM match is found.

- **Analyze Files**: You may wish to run this task repeatedly during large projects so that you can gauge your progress at different stages via the **Analyze Files** report. It is useful in a project context to set the option **Report internal fuzzy match leverage**, to see how many fuzzy matches are produced by the project files themselves rather than by the TM. Translators may, however, want to exercise caution when using this option for analysis, since it forms the basis for a quotation or invoice: revealing to the customer the similarities within the file itself may encourage the customer to negotiate for a lower fee.

Finding and replacing text in multiple SDLXLIFFs

The **SDL Batch Find and Replace** tool is an SDL OpenExchange app that gets installed along with SDL Trados Studio. It enables you to find and replace text in selected or all SDLXLIFFs in a project.

To open the tool, go to the **Welcome** view and select it from the list at the top left, as shown in the following screenshot:

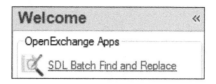

To add a selection of SDLXLIFFs in which to find and replace text, in the **Files** tab, choose **Add** and select the files from the project folder. You will find the SDLXLIFFs in the target folder (which has a name such as `fr-FR` or `en-US`).

 If you are unsure where to find the project folder, before you add the files, in the **Files** view, right-click the name of a file in the project and choose **Explore Containing Folder**. Rather than trying to remember the file path, you can copy its path from the address bar in Windows Explorer and paste it back when you add the files in **SDL Batch Find and Replace**.

To add all the SDLXLIFFs in a project, in the **Files** tab, choose **Load files from Project**, and select the project (`.sdlproj`) file. When prompted, select the target language(s) for the find and replace operation. You can then use the **Find** and **Replace** tabs to specify various parameters for finding and replacing text across the selected SDLXLIFFs.

Following a replace operation, you will see a **Replace Results** window highlighting the changes in their segment context, as shown in the following screenshot:

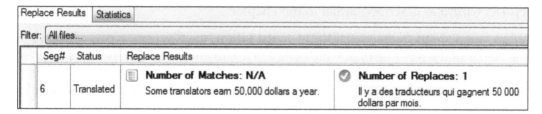

To see how many instances were replaced in each file, click on the **Statistics** tab, shown in the following screenshot:

Search Results	Project	Matches in Target	Replaced	Warnings
N:¥packt¥2014¥Chap 7¥Chapter 7 demo project¥fr-FR¥configuration documenta...		0	0	0
N:¥packt¥2014¥Chap 7¥Chapter 7 demo project¥fr-FR¥configuration documenta...		2	2	0

Bear in mind that the TMs will not be updated with any changed segments. You can update the TMs separately using, for example, the **Update Main Translation Memories** batch task, described earlier.

Merging files into one SDLXLIFF

If you are working with a number of smaller, or very similar, project files, it can often be beneficial to merge them during or after project creation so that you can translate and review them in a single SDLXLIFF. This has several advantages: you save the time of opening and closing lots of small files, and you can compare document contexts (in the **Display Filter**, for example). You can also use auto-propagation and find and replace text across different files. There are two ways to merge files, described in the following sections.

Merging files during project creation

To merge files during project creation, in the **Project Files** screen of the new project wizard, add the files and select those that you want to merge, and then click the **Merge Files** button. In the **Merge Files** window, in the **Merged file name** field, type in a name for the merged SDLXLIFF and click **OK**, and complete the **New Project** wizard as described earlier in this chapter.

When you open the merged SDLXLIFF in the **Editor**, the Navigation pane displays the names of the separate files, which you can use to jump between them. Once open, the merged files retain their original segment numbers. To jump between segments with the same number, find them with **Go To** (*Ctrl* + *G*), and then use **Previous** and **Next** (*Ctrl* + *J*) to move between different segments with the same number.

The segments in the **Editor** are separated by the filenames, as shown in the following screenshot:

15	• Merging·smaller·files·into·a·single·bilingual·Tr
	new product presentation.ppt configuration documentation part 2.docx
1	**Translating·sentences**

When you run **Generate Target Translations** on a merged SDLXLIFF, the translated documents are generated as the original, separate files.

Merging files on the fly with QuickMerge

Most usefully, it is possible to select files in an existing project from the list in the **Files** view to merge on the fly. This offers all the advantages of merging files during project creation, described in the previous section, but creates a *virtually* merged SDLXLIFF, which disappears as soon as you close it. This feature is called **QuickMerge**.

Translator *Emma Goldsmith* sums up the usefulness of QuickMerge nicely in her blog article on this feature at `http://tinyurl.com/quickmerge`:

> *The other day I wanted to change something in a set of files I'd translated, but I couldn't remember which file it was in. I opened them all with QuickMerge and found it immediately with Ctrl + F.*

To merge files with QuickMerge, select them in the list in the **Files** view, and press *Enter*. This opens the merged files in Translation mode. To open them in Review or Sign-off mode, select the files and then, from the **Open** group or right-click menu, select **Open For Review** or **Open For Sign-off**.

Adjacent files selected with the *Shift* key are merged in the order in the list. To change the order, you can first re-order them by clicking on the relevant header, for example alphabetically or by date or size. Alternatively, simply select them one by one in the desired order with *Ctrl* + left mouse clicks.

If you generate the target files from a QuickMerge file via **Save Target As**, you are prompted to save the original files individually. Note that you cannot use QuickMerge to open files already merged during project creation.

Tools for project managers

In this section, we discuss a number of project-related features that are primarily of interest to project managers, but which are also useful for translators to know about.

PerfectMatch

PerfectMatch is a more reliable version of context matching for use in situations where the source documents are updated, either periodically or during translation (as is common in localization projects). If a client sends an updated source document without indicating what has changed, you may feel the need to recheck even segments with a 100% match from the TM to make sure that wider changes in the context do not require a change in the translation. PerfectMatch addresses this problem by checking the document context of each segment against the corresponding segment in the originally translated bilingual (SDLXLIFF or TTX) file, rather than against the TMs, to provide a strongly context-based match.

> PerfectMatch segments can only be created in the Professional version. Users of the Freelance version can display PerfectMatch segments in SDLXLIFFs given to them by other users, and use them in the **Display Filter**, for example, but they cannot create them.

PerfectMatch segments can be generated during project creation, as described in this section, or on one or more files in an existing project, via **Batch Tasks | Apply PerfectMatch**. PerfectMatch segments appear in a separate category in the **Analyze Files** report, for inclusion in or exclusion from the billable word count, as desired.

The easiest way to create a PerfectMatch project is to re-use the settings from the original project (before the source documents were updated):

1. In the **Projects** view, go the **Home** tab and choose **New Project**.

2. In the **Project Type** screen, choose **Create a project based on a previous project**, and select your original project from the list, as shown in the following screenshot. If it does not appear in the list, click **Browse** and, from your original project folder, select the project file (extension `.sdlproj`).

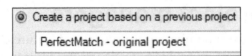

3. Follow the wizard. When you get to the **Project Files** screen, add the updated source documents as the files for translation in this project. You should be able to leave all other settings unchanged, because they will have been picked up from the original project. Continue until you reach the **SDL PerfectMatch** screen.

4. In the **SDL PerfectMatch** screen, you will see that any documents whose filename has not been changed have been paired up with the SDLXLIFF file from the original project to provide PerfectMatch segments based on their original document context. In the example shown in the following screenshot in step 5, the first file in the list has been renamed (from **v1.0** to **v2.0**), and so has not been paired, but both the other two files have been paired automatically.

5. To pair an unpaired file in the list, right-click in the area under **Previous Document** and select **Add Previous Document** as shown in the following screenshot, and browse to the original project folder:

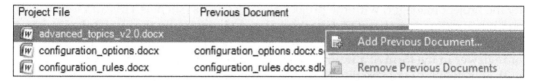

6. You will need to locate the target folder created by SDL Trados Studio (it will have a name such as `fr-FR` or `en-US`). From the target folder, select the corresponding SDLXLIFF or TTX file. In our example in the preceding screenshot, this is the file named `advanced_topics_v1.0.docx.sdlxliff`. Leave the **Translation transfer options** setting at the bottom of the screen as **Apply PerfectMatch and lock**.

7. Once all of the PerfectMatch file pairs are in place, go through the rest of the project wizard as normally.

In the new SDLXLIFF, PerfectMatch segments have the **PM** segment type, signed off status, and are locked with the text grayed out, as shown in the following screenshot:

For more details, see the PerfectMatch help files at `http://tinyurl.com/perf-match`.

Project packages

Project packages are a tool for project managers to share some or all of the files and the settings in a project with a translator or reviewer by placing those files and settings in one file (the project package) that can easily be delivered by e-mail, FTP, and so on.

In the Freelance version, project packages can be opened but not created. The instructions in this section on creating a project package are therefore only relevant to users of the Professional version of SDL Trados Studio.

How project packages work

Project packages are created from a project configured by the project manager to send to a translator or reviewer. When the translator or reviewer receives the project package and opens it in SDL Trados Studio, the project will appear exactly as set up by the project manager, with the project files, resources (such as TMs and termbases), and other settings (such as **QA Checker**) already in place. By the same token, when the project manager opens the translated or reviewed files sent back by the translator or reviewer in the form of a return package, the project files will have been updated with any changes made by the translator or reviewer, and should import back into and update the original project. The project manager can then, if necessary, use the same project to create another project package in which to send the material to another participant in the project cycle.

Creating a project package

The following is a summary of the procedure for creating a project package:

1. In the **Projects** view, select the project and, from the **Home** tab or right-click menu, choose **Create Project Package** (or if the package recipient is using SDL Trados Studio 2009, **Create Project Trados 2009 Package**).

Projects and project packages created in SDL Trados Studio 2011/2014 cannot be opened in SDL Trados Studio 2009, although those created in SDL Trados Studio 2009 can be opened in SDL Trados Studio 2011/2014.

2. In the **Select Files** screen, select the project files to include by ticking the box(es) under **Name**.

3. In the **Project Package Options** screen, specify the target folder where the package will be created. If your project has more than one target language, you can also specify whether to create a separate package for each one.

4. In the **Review Project Packages** screen, you must assign the project package to a user under **Assign to**. To create a user, click **Users**. Assigned users do not have to be real people; you can use aliases such as "Translator (En-Fr)" if you prefer.

You must also choose a **Task** from **Translate** or **Review**. This setting determines whether the files will open in Translation or Review mode when opened by the recipient. If you add entries to **Due date** and **Comment**, they will be seen by the recipient when the package is opened.

An example of these settings is shown in the following screenshot:

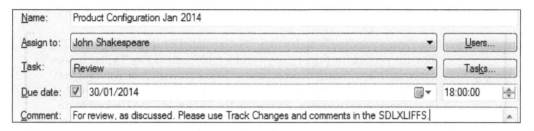

5. The **Additional Options** screen allows you to specify the material that is included in the package. Under **Project Translation Memory**, if you do not want the translator or reviewer to work with project TMs, select **Do not include any project translation memories** (see the section later in this chapter for an explanation of project TMs). Under **File-based Resources**, choose the TMs and other resources that you want to include.

   Click **Finish** to create the project package.

6. To access the project package (.sdlppx file) so that you can send it to the intended recipient, in the **Creating Packages** screen, click **Open Target Folder**.

Opening a project package

To open a project package that you have received from your project manager, choose **File | Open Package**. When you select the package, you will first see the **Review Package Contents** screen displaying a list of the files for translation or review, word count information, and any comments from the project manager. Under **Project Folder**, specify a target folder to store the project, and then click **Finish** (if the project package was created in SDL Trados Studio 2009, you will be prompted to choose the target folder after you click **Finish**). Wait until the project has imported and click **Close**. The project now appears in the list of projects in the **Projects** view.

Project packages are also commonly used in **SDL Worldserver** and **SDL TMS** environments. Users can open and process SDL Worldserver or SDL TMS packages in SDL Trados Studio as normally (such as by adding local termbases and TMs of their own). Return packages have to be created by the same ID/person who opened them. Each saves back to the appropriate format for upload to SDL Worldserver or SDL TMS.

Returning translated or reviewed files

To return the translated or reviewed files to your project manager, you will create a **return package** to send to your project manager. In the **Projects** view, select the project and, from the **Home** tab or right-click menu, choose **Create Return Package**. Follow the instructions in the wizard, specifying the location for your return package (the `.sdlrpx` file).

The return package includes only the translated or reviewed SDLXLIFF files, the project file (`.sdlproj`), and a folder called **File Types**. It does not contain any translation resources (TMs, termbases, or AutoSuggest dictionaries). Once the translations in the SDLXLIFFs are considered final, the project manager can update the TMs using the **Update Main Translation Memories** batch task, as described earlier in this chapter.

Opening a return package

To open a return package from a translator or reviewer, choose **File | Open Package** and follow the instructions in the wizard. This will update the SDLXLIFF files in the *original project* on which the project package is based with the translated or reviewed versions.

The return package can therefore only be opened in an instance of SDL Trados Studio in which the original project is open. If the original project was created on a different person's machine, for example, you must open the project (`.sdlproj`) file on your own machine first (by copying the entire project folder, or over a network, for example).

About project translation memories

In SDL Trados Studio, the TMs that you create and select to use in a project are known as **main translation memories**. A **project translation memory**, on the other hand, is a *subset* of a main TM that is sometimes used in project management situations. To create a project TM, SDL Trados Studio compares the main TMs selected for use in the project against the project files. Only those segments in the main TMs that will produce a match in the project files are then extracted and placed in a separate project TM.

Imagine a project manager with a large TM containing far more material than is relevant to the documents needing translation. Rather than passing the entire TM to the translator, he can instead generate a smaller project TM containing only matching segments.

A negative consequence of this is that project TMs may, in some cases, prevent the translator from finding potential sub-segment matches via a concordance search. It is therefore good project management practice to provide freelance translators and reviewers with larger memories for such sub-matches, thus helping to maintain consistency with clients' terminology.

Note that when the translation is done using a project TM, the project TM gets updated, but the main TM from which it was created does not, even if it is set to update. This is because project TMs are partly intended to be a means for the project manager to ensure that the main TM does not get updated until the translations have been approved. Freelance translators who use a project TM can add a separate TM to the existing project, in which to store their translations and generate matches as they work.

To use project translation memories, in the **Project Preparation** screen of the **New Project** wizard, choose the task **Prepare** instead of **Prepare without project TM**.

A project translation memory is generated for each main translation memory in a subfolder of the project folder, named **Tm**.

Project translation memories appear as follows in the **Project Settings** window:

Name	Enabled	Lookup	Penalty	Concordance	Update
tm product config.sdltm	☑	☑	0	☑	☑
Product configuration V2_tm product config.sdl..	☑				

Summary

In this chapter, you learned various techniques for creating and working with projects and project packages to manage and exchange translation documents, and the resources and settings associated with them. In the following chapter, we look at how to get matches from text inside segments by working with terminology databases.

8
Managing Terminology

Termbases are a great way to boost the number of matches you get from your TMs by storing terminology and other chunks of text that appear inside various segments in different contexts, and do not therefore always produce a match from the TM. Termbase matches are recognized and displayed automatically by SDL Trados Studio without the need to search, and you can insert them into your target segment at the press of a key or button. Termbases are created in SDL MultiTerm, which is the terminology component of SDL Trados Studio.

 MultiTerm is not available as part of the trial version of SDL Trados Studio. You will need access to a licensed version of SDL Trados Studio to use it.

Managing terminology in MultiTerm

To get the best out of MultiTerm, it is a good idea to familiarize yourself with the way it organizes terminology before you start using it.

Some translators use termbases to store and instantly match not just terminology per se, but any string of text that appears frequently in different segment contexts, whether it is a common collocation or a technical term. This is not the traditional approach to using termbases, but it can speed up your work by helping you to avoid retyping text strings that occur frequently in the material that you are translating.

Essential information about MultiTerm termbases

Unlike file-based TMs, MultiTerm termbases can include more than two languages. When you select a termbase for use during translation, SDL Trados Studio will automatically pick out the language pair that matches your bilingual document. You do not need to specify sublanguages. For example, the termbase language French will give termbase matches for bilingual documents whose language is either French (France) or French (Canada).

In a MultiTerm termbase, a field containing meta-information about terms, such as a definition, note, or examples of usage, is referred to as a **descriptive** field.

Descriptive field information can be added to term entries and displayed back on three levels known as entry classes, shown in the following screenshot, and explained following the screenshot. This knowledge is indispensable when you create and interact with a termbase.

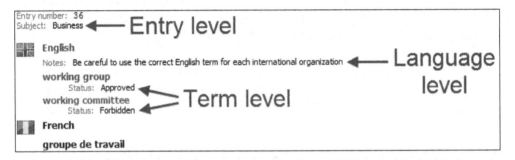

The entry classes in MultiTerm term entries are as follows:

- **Entry level**: Information that applies equally to all of the languages and all of the terms (including any synonyms) in the entry. In our example, the field **Subject** is assumed to be the same no matter what the language, and to apply equally to any terms and their synonyms that appear in the entry, so that the subject **Business** covers all of the terms under both **English** and **French**, and any other languages.

- **Language (or index) level**: Information that applies to one of the languages, including any synonyms in that language, but not to the other languages. The information under **English** in the **Notes** field applies to both **English** synonyms, but not to the **French** entry.

- **Term level**: Information that applies to a particular term but not to its synonyms. The **English** synonyms **working group** and **working committee** have been given different statuses to guide translators as to which term to use.

Creating a simple termbase

This section takes you through the process of creating a simple termbase in MultiTerm, focusing on the key knowledge required at each stage.

 To create a termbase, you must use MultiTerm. Once it is created, you can open it in SDL Trados Studio, from where you can add entries to it and use it to recognize and display matches automatically during translation.

To create a termbase in MultiTerm, perform the following steps:

1. To open MultiTerm on Windows 7, choose **Start | All Programs | SDL | SDL MultiTerm 2014 | SDL MultiTerm 2014 Desktop** (or double-click the icon on your desktop). On Windows 8, click the SDL MultiTerm Studio 2014 icon on the desktop or the Metro screen.

2. In MultiTerm, choose **File | New** and, on the right, click **Create Termbase** (or press *Ctrl + Alt + T* from anywhere else except the **File** tab) as shown in the following screenshot:

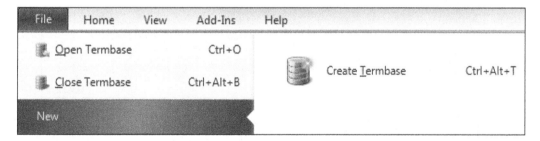

3. When prompted, save the termbase under an appropriate name and folder with the extension `.sdltb`, and then, in the **Termbase Wizard**, click **Next**.

4. In the **Termbase Definition** screen, you will choose a termbase definition. This defines the structure of the termbase (including what languages, descriptive fields, and entry classes the termbase contains, and how they interrelate). Choose **Create a new termbase definition from scratch**, as shown in the following screenshot:

 Alternatively, **Use a predefined template | Multilingual glossary** gives a preconfigured termbase definition that can be modified in the wizard and is a good way to get going quickly or experiment when you are new to MultiTerm.

5. In the **Termbase Name** screen, type a **Friendly Name**. This is the name by which the termbase will be displayed later when you select it in SDL Trados Studio and MultiTerm, so make sure it identifies your termbase properly. It is generally a good idea to use the same name as the one that you entered as the filename for the termbase.

6. In the **Language Fields** screen, add the desired languages by choosing a language in the list and clicking **Add**, as shown in the following screenshot. Repeat this process for each language that you want to add, and then click **Next**.

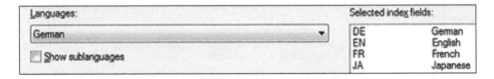

7. In the **Descriptive Fields** screen, add the desired fields. In our example, we add a **Notes** field to allow us to freely add any desired information about the entry, and a **Subject** field that will contain a predefined list of subject areas, as shown in the following screenshot:

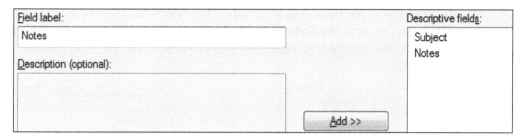

To create a field for entering any desired text: Under **Field label**, type the name of the field (such as Notes) and click **Add**. Descriptive fields are set, by default, to have the data type **Text**, which means that you can type in any combination of text, numbers, or other characters in that field when you create term entries later on.

To create a predefined list: Under **Field label**, type the name of the field (such as Subject) and click **Add**. On the right, select the name of the newly added field and click **Properties**. From the **Data type** list, choose **Picklist**. To add a new item to the picklist, click the green plus symbol button, double-click in the first row below **Picklist**, type a name for the item (such as Business), and press *Enter*, as shown in the following screenshot. Repeat this process for each item that you want to add. When you add another entry to this list, you will not need to double-click in the row, as the cursor will already have moved down ready for you to type the next entry.

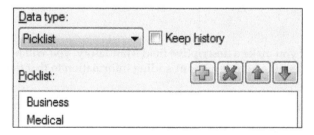

8. Click **OK** to return to the **Descriptive Fields** screen. When you have set up all of the desired descriptive fields, click **Next**.

9. In the **Entry Structure** screen, shown in the following screenshot, you will decide the level at which you want your descriptive fields to be available to add and display information. On the right, in the **Available descriptive fields** pane, select a descriptive field. On the left, in the **Entry Structure** pane, select the desired entry class, and click **Add**. If you have placed a descriptive field at the wrong level and want to remove it, select the descriptive field on the left-hand side and click **Remove** to move it back to the **Available descriptive fields** pane.

In the example in the following screenshot, the **Notes** field has been added at all three levels, and the **Subject** field at **Entry level** only. See the preceding section, *Essential information about MultiTerm termbases*, for the logic behind these choices.

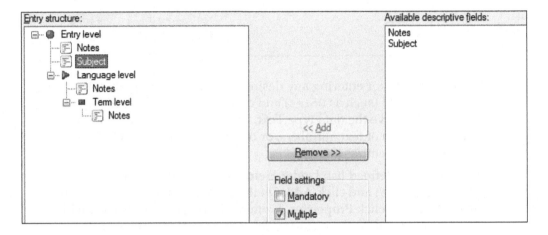

10. If you are adding a picklist field, you can choose whether or not to allow the selection of multiple options from the list (for example, if a term belongs in both **Business** and **Medical** subject areas). Under **Entry structure**, select the name of the field, and then, under **Field settings**, select **Multiple**. Otherwise, you will only be able to select one picklist option when adding entries to the termbase.

 If you make a descriptive field **Mandatory**, you will not be able to save an entry without adding information to that field.

11. In the **Wizard Complete** screen, click **Finish** to create the termbase.

Modifying an existing termbase

To modify your termbase definition after creation, such as if you want to add more languages, or new options to a picklist, you must open the termbase in MultiTerm.

In MultiTerm, choose **File | Open Termbase** (*Ctrl + O*), and at the bottom left, click the **Termbase Management** button shown in the following screenshot:

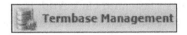

In the **Catalog Categories** window shown in the following screenshot, under the name of the termbase, select **Definition**, and then from the **Home** tab or right-click menu, choose **Edit**:

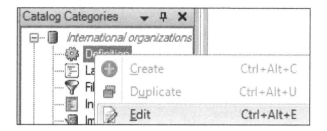

This opens a wizard similar to that used to create the termbase. Follow the wizard and make your changes.

 It is generally possible to add fields and information to your termbase definition, but you will not be able to remove fields that already contain information.

Using termbases in SDL Trados Studio

Once you have created a termbase in MultiTerm, you can open it in SDL Trados Studio so that you can add entries and get matches from the termbase during translation.

Selecting termbases in SDL Trados Studio

In the **Editor** view, with a document open in Translation mode, the **Term Recognition** window at the top right initially indicates that there is no termbase open, as shown in the following screenshot:

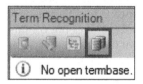

To select a termbase to use during translation, perform the following steps:

1. To open a termbase, click the **Project Termbase Settings** button on the right of the toolbar (highlighted in the preceding screenshot). In the **Termbases** pane of the **Project Settings** dialog box, click **Add**. In the **Select Termbases** dialog box, click **Browse** and select one or more termbases. The selected termbases then appear in a list identified by their friendly name. Each has a checkbox by which it can be selected or deselected for use, as shown in the following screenshot:

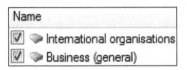

2. Click **OK** to add the termbases to the list in the **Termbases** pane of the **Project Settings** dialog box, as shown in the following screenshot:

Entries that you add to a termbase while translating in SDL Trados Studio are added only to the termbase marked **default**, which is always the one at the top of the list. The other termbases will provide matches but not receive new term entries. To change the default termbase, use the **Move Up** and **Move Down** buttons, or **Set Default** button, on the right.

3. Click **OK** to open the termbase(s) for use during translation.

 If the **Term Recognition** window displays the text **No results available**, this means that there is at least one open termbase, but that the termbase does not contain any matches for the segment active in the **Editor**.

Using termbases during translation

In this section, we will describe several ways to add entries to a termbase and to insert termbase matches in your target segments efficiently as you translate.

Adding entries to a termbase during translation

First use your mouse to select the text in both the source and target segments, as shown in the following screenshot:

To add the entry to the default termbase, right-click the selected phrase and choose **Add new term**, or press *Ctrl + F2*. The source and target terms now appear in editable mode on the left of the **Editor** in the **Termbase Viewer** pane (which is minimized until you create a new termbase entry).

 Sometimes, messages relating to the user's Java setup can appear at this point. For information on this issue, see the SDL Knowledgebase article at http://tinyurl.com/multiterm-java.

To edit a term entry before you add it to the termbase, double-click in the term field to expand it as shown in the following screenshot, and edit the text:

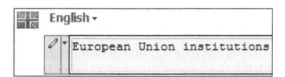

To finish editing the term, click anywhere in the **Termbase Viewer** pane outside the term field or press *Enter*. You can also use the *Tab* key to jump between the fields of the editing form.

To add information to a descriptive field, click the down arrow icon at the appropriate entry level (**entry**, **language**, or **term**), and select the descriptive field from the list. In the following screenshot, we are adding information to the **Subject** field at entry level:

To finish editing the descriptive field, click anywhere in the **Termbase Viewer** pane outside the descriptive field or press *Enter*.

To add a synonym, click the down arrow icon next to the language name and choose **Term**.

To remove a descriptive field, click the name of the descriptive field and press *Delete*.

To add the entry to the termbase, you must save it by clicking the **Save this Entry** button or pressing *Ctrl + F12*. Note that the entry is not added to the termbase until you save it.

To edit an existing entry, on the left of the **Termbase Viewer** pane, select the term in the list, and click the **Edit this Entry** button or press *F2*. If the **Termbase Viewer** pane is not displayed, from the **View** tab, choose **Termbase Viewer**.

You can close the **Termbase Viewer** pane when you are not using it to add or edit entries. In Translation mode, it will reappear automatically each time you add a new entry. If you have more than one termbase open, the **Termbase Viewer** displays the default termbase.

To open **Termbase Viewer** with terms displayed in the **Term Recognition** window as matching entries for the segment that is active in the side-by-side Editor, select the entry in the **Term Recognition** window, right-click, and choose **View term details**.

Inserting termbase matches into your translation

Termbase matches are displayed by a red line over the corresponding text in the source segment, as with the two entries **European Union institutions** and **open competition** shown in the following screenshot:

The European Union institutions normally recruit translators through an open competition.

The entries also appear in the **Term Recognition** window. If there is more than one termbase, the name of the termbase that produces the match appears on the right of the source term as in the following screenshot:

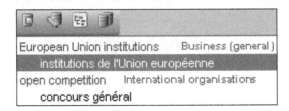

The buttons at the top of the screenshot are, from left to right, **View term details**, **Insert term translation**, **Hitlist settings**, and **Project Termbase Settings**. We will refer to these buttons in the explanations later in this chapter.

> Term entries are matched based on fuzzy recognition, so the word `apple` in your segment should produce a match based on the termbase entry `apples`. The minimum match level is set under **Project Settings | Language Pairs | All Language Pairs | Termbases | Seach Settings | Minimum match value**.

Three ways to insert terms

In each of the following methods, position the cursor at the appropriate point in the target segment first.

- **AutoSuggest method**: Type the first letter of the entry in the target language. You will be given a list of AutoSuggest matches, including termbase entries beginning with that letter. AutoSuggest matches can come from any AutoSuggest dictionaries or AutoText entries that you are working with, as well as from the termbase. The following screenshot shows an AutoSuggest list with matches from the termbase (at the top) and the AutoSuggest dictionary, represented by different icons:

To insert the termbase entry, double-click it in the list, or select it and press *Enter*.

> To make best use of the AutoSuggest method, it is best not to add entries beginning with articles such as "the" and "a" to the termbase, because the articles will then form the first letters of the entries, making it more difficult for you to select the term that you want.

AutoSuggest matches are, by default, not case sensitive. This means that if you type the first letter as a capital, the entry is inserted with an initial capital, even if the entry in the termbase does not itself begin with a capital letter.

If the same entry occurs more than once in the segment and no AutoSuggest match is produced after you insert it the first time, choose **File | Options | AutoSuggest** and uncheck the option **Hide suggestions which have already been used**.

- **Shortcut method**: The shortcut *Ctrl + Shift + L* produces a list of termbase entries for the segment, as shown in the following screenshot. To insert the term, double-click it in the list, or select it and press *Enter*.

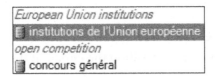

- **Mouse method**: In the **Term Recognition** window, select the target term and click the **Insert term translation** button.

Configuring how termbase matches are displayed

Descriptive field information is, by default, not displayed alongside termbase matches in the **Term Recognition** window. To change this behavior, in the **Term Recognition** window, click the **Hitlist settings** button, choose **Select fields**, and select the descriptive fields that you want to appear. In the following screenshot, we select the **Subject** field at entry level and the **Notes** fields that appear by the terms themselves:

An entry for which we have selected an option from the **Subject** list and entered some text in the **Note** field against the target term will appear in the **Term Recognition** window as in the following screenshot:

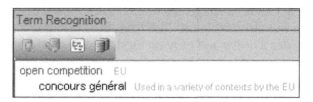

Converting terminology between MultiTerm and Excel

In this section, we show you how to convert a simple Excel glossary into a MultiTerm termbase and vice versa. There are two options for converting terminology from glossaries into MultiTerm. One is the **Glossary Converter** app that users with a valid SDL Trados Studio license can download from the SDL OpenExchange App Store, and the other is the **MultiTerm Convert** tool that is included with the standard MultiTerm installation.

Glossary Converter allows you to convert terminology between MultiTerm termbases and Excel glossaries. It creates a new termbase when converting terminology from an Excel glossary, but does not allow you to import term lists to an existing termbase. MultiTerm Convert, on the other hand, allows you to convert glossaries from various formats into MultiTerm, but not to export out of MultiTerm. MultiTerm Convert is arguably more complex to use than Glossary Converter, but gives users correspondingly more control over the import process, and allows you to add term lists to an existing glossary (provided that the structure of the glossary is similar enough to that of the termbase). For most freelance users, however, Glossary Converter is likely to be sufficient for their needs.

Note that flat file formats such as Excel files are not designed to handle the kind of complex, cross-field relations that database files such as termbases can manage, so some preparation and experimentation may be required to get the conversion to work as you want it to. Whichever tool you use, a number of files are created automatically in the conversion process, so it is a good idea to create a copy of the glossary that you are converting in a new, separate folder.

Glossary Converter tool

The Glossary Converter tool is especially useful for freelancers working with simple glossaries. If you have a valid SDL Trados Studio license, you can download the app from the SDL OpenExchange site `http://www.translationzone.com/openexchange`. You can also access this link from the **Welcome** view's Navigation pane. The app provides a quick and easy method to convert glossaries in spreadsheet format (`.xls`, `.xlsx`, `.csv`, or `.txt`) to a MultiTerm termbase and vice versa. The examples described in this chapter were performed in Version 3.0 of the app.

For more information about the various conversion options in Glossary Converter, visit the developer's support pages at `http://tinyurl.com/glossary-converter`.

Preparing your terminology before import

Before converting your glossary, ensure that each column in the Excel file has an identifiable heading, as the column headings will form the names of the language fields and descriptive fields in the converted termbase.

When preparing a glossary for conversion in Glossary Converter, consider the following possibilities:

- **To import synonyms**: To import synonyms, separate the synonyms in each language column using (by default) the | (pipe) symbol. In the following screenshot showing part of a glossary, the **English** entry outlined in the first row contains two synonyms separated in this way.

- **To add information in descriptive fields**: One area that requires careful thought is how to add to your Excel glossary information that will appear in the termbase in the form of a descriptive field (see the *Essential information about MultiTerm termbases* section earlier in this chapter).

   To add descriptive field information at entry level, we create a single column that applies to all of the other information in that particular row in the Excel file. In the following screenshot, the **Subject** column will become a field at entry level after conversion.

   To add information at **language (index)** or **term** level, we create separate descriptive fields for each language or synonym respectively. In the following screenshot, we have created separate **Gender** columns corresponding to each of the **French** and **German** columns, to allow for the fact that the two languages will have different gender information. Columns other than languages are assigned to the language column on their left during conversion, so we can expect the two gender columns to be assigned to the correct languages in the converted termbase.

Subject	English	French	Gender	German	Gender
EU	working group | working committee	groupe de travail	Masc	Arbeitsgruppe	Fem
EU	European Commission	Commission européenne	Fem	Europäische Behörde	Fem

At the time of writing, descriptive fields are converted into the text field type. There is no simple way to convert, for example, the **Gender** field in the glossary in the preceding screenshot into a picklist field in the termbase. Instead, the entries (such as **Masc** and **Fem**) will appear in the termbase as text inside a text field. A workaround for this, which is beyond the scope of this book, is to use a termbase template to perform the conversion. See the developer's support pages for more details.

- **Assigning descriptive fields to synonyms**: A further complication arises when you have synonyms that each require different descriptive field information assigning to them, such as when you have synonyms with a different gender or status. This issue is also dealt with using (by default) the | (pipe) symbol, as shown in the following screenshot:

English	Status	French	Status
working group | task force | working committee	Forbidden | | Approved	groupe de travail | force opérationnelle	Forbidden | Approved

Here, the **English** entry contains three synonyms and the **French** two. The status for each synonym is assigned by separating the statuses with the pipe symbol. In the **English** entry, no status is assigned to the middle of the three synonyms by leaving empty the place between the two pipe symbols where the status would appear.

Converting from Excel to MultiTerm

First we will show you how to convert an Excel glossary into a termbase:

1. In Windows 7, go to **Start** | **All Programs** | **SDL OpenExchange**, choose **GlossaryConverter**. In Windows 8, choose **Start** and go to the **Apps** list (Metro screen), then choose **Glossary Converter**. A shortcut is also added automatically to your desktop, and you can add a shortcut to your taskbar.

2. Open Windows Explorer at the location containing the glossary, and drag and drop the glossary file into the **Glossary Converter** window, shown in the following screenshot, or onto the shortcut icon:

Notice that the gray frames around the Glossary Converter interface change color while the conversion is being processed, and a progress bar runs at the bottom.

3. If your Glossary Converter settings are prepared correctly (see **Glossary Converter** support pages for further explanations), Glossary Converter uses the column headings from the Excel file to assign the columns to fields in the termbase.

In Glossary Converter, you will see that the column headers from your Excel file are now listed under **Name**. Check that each field under **Name** has the correct field type assigned to it under **Field Type**. Under **Language**, Glossary Converter lists the language that MultiTerm will assign in the converted termbase to the language columns from the Excel file. Check that the termbase languages (under **Language**) are all paired with the correct language from the Excel file (under **Name**).

If any of the information is incorrect, or if Glossary Converter initially shows the word **Unknown** under **Field Type**, as shown in the following screenshot, select the row and click the appropriate button on the right to assign or change the language, or to define the level at which the field should appear in the termbase:

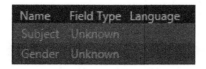

 Glossary Converter stores the column names and associated field type that you import, so that it can assign the same field type information to those column names the next time you convert a glossary. To check or modify this information, click the **settings** area of the Glossary Converter window and choose the **Fields** tab at the top. Here, you can add and delete entries and modify their file type and language associations.

4. If all of the **Field Type** information is correct, click the **OK** button. The glossary will be converted into a MultiTerm termbase and various settings files in the same folder as the glossary. Note that if you have previously converted a glossary with the same column headers, Glossary Converter may remember all of the column information and create the converted termbase in your folder without showing you the screen in the preceding screenshot.

Converting from MultiTerm to Excel

Glossary Converter is currently the easiest way to convert a MultiTerm termbase into a spreadsheet format. The procedure is very similar to that described in the preceding section. Simply drag your termbase (.sdltb) file onto the **Glossary Converter** window, make any necessary changes to the settings in the **Field Definition** screen, and click **OK**. The glossary is created in the same folder as the termbase in .xlsx format.

Converting glossaries with MultiTerm Convert

Converting glossaries with MultiTerm Convert can be slightly daunting at first, but with practice, you should find that you can do it fairly quickly. Conversion with MultiTerm Convert is a three-stage process, described in the following sections. MultiTerm Convert can convert glossaries from a number of formats, but we will focus on conversion from Excel-based glossaries.

Preparing your terminology before import

Before importing, prepare your glossary in a similar way to that described previously for the Glossary Converter tool. To import synonyms, however, you must create an additional column with exactly the same language name, as in the case of the two **English** columns in the following screenshot:

English	English	French	Gender	German	Gender
working group	working committee	groupe de travail	Masc	Arbeitsgruppe	Fem
European Commission		Commission européenne	Fem	Europäische Behörde	Fem

Stage 1 – running MultiTerm Convert

The first step in this three-stage process is to use MultiTerm Convert to split your glossary into two parts: content (filename ending in .mtf.xml) and structure (filename ending in .xdt).

1. To open MultiTerm Convert, in Windows 7, choose **Start | All Programs | SDL | SDL MultiTerm 2014 | SDL MultiTerm 2014 Convert**. In Windows 8, go to the **Apps/Metro** screen and choose **SDL MultiTerm 2014 Convert**.

   This opens a wizard.

2. In the first screen titled **Welcome**, click **Next**. In the screen titled **Conversion Session**, leave the default option (**New conversion session**) checked and click **Next**.

> Getting the conversion right can, in some cases, take trial and error, by running the conversion process several times until you get it right. To avoid reconfiguring the settings in the wizard each time, you can save your settings by checking the option **Save conversion session** and then clicking **Save as** to save the conversion file (.xcd). The next time you run the conversion on the same glossary, choose **Load existing conversion session**, select the conversion session file, and then go through the wizard as shown in the following steps, tweaking the settings as necessary.

3. In the screen titled **Conversion Options**, select **Microsoft Excel format** as the format of the glossary file you want to import, as shown in the following screenshot, and then click **Next**:

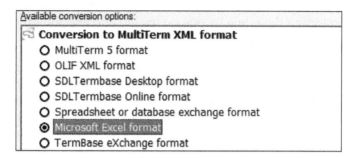

4. In the screen titled **Specify Files**, click the first **Browse** button next to the **Input file** field and select your Excel glossary. The other fields are then filled out automatically. Click **Next**.

5. In the screen titled **Specify Column Header**, on the left, select a column header, and on the right, assign it either as **Language field** (selecting the appropriate language from the list), or **Descriptive field** (selecting the appropriate data type from the list). Do this for all column headers, one by one.

    In the following screenshot, we assign the termbase language **German** (on the right) to the column in the Excel file with the header **German** (on the left). We assign the column headers **English** and **French** in the same way, by selecting them on the left and choosing the appropriate **Language field** on the right.

    For the column header **Gender**, we select it on the left, click the option **Descriptive field** on the right, and choose **Picklist** from the list, as shown in the following screenshot:

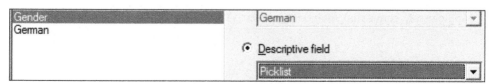

In our example, the picklist values **Masc** and **Fem** from the Excel glossary will be placed in the picklist automatically when we import the terms in Stage 3 of this process. Once you have finished assigning all of the column headers, you can check that you have assigned them to the correct termbase field by selecting them one by one on the left and checking the termbase field that you have assigned them to on the right.

6. In the screen titled **Create Entry Structure**, we add the descriptive fields on the right to the appropriate entry class on the left. In our example, reflecting the two **Gender** columns in our Excel file, we assign **Gender #1** to the **French** term, and **Gender #2** to the **German** term, as shown in the following screenshot. Notice that there are two entries for English, because the Excel glossary in our example contains two columns for that language to store the synonyms.

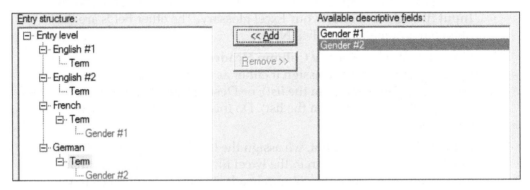

7. Click **Next** in the remaining screens of the wizard. You will see a message telling you the number of entries converted followed by the **Conversion Complete** screen. Click **Finish**.

In the folder that contains your glossary, these steps will have created three additional files with the same name as your glossary, shown in the following screenshot. Of these, the .xdt and .mtf.xml files will be used in the next two stages.

glossary_conversion_multiterm_convert_V1.log	Text Document
glossary_conversion_multiterm_convert_V1.mtf.xml	XML File
glossary_conversion_multiterm_convert_V1.xdt	XDT File
glossary_conversion_multiterm_convert_V1.xlsx	Microsoft Excel Worksheet

Stage 2 – creating a new termbase from your structure file

It is possible to import terminology lists into a preexisting termbase, but the structures of the termbase and the imported file must be compatible for this to work. To simplify our explanation, we will create a new termbase to import into. If you are importing into a preexisting MultiTerm termbase, you can skip this step and go straight to Stage 3.

The process of creating the termbase in MultiTerm is as described earlier in this chapter in the *Creating a simple termbase* section, but there is now one difference.

In the **Termbase Definition** screen, to ensure that your new termbase has the same structure as your glossary, you will choose the termbase definition file created by MultiTerm Convert in Stage 1. Choose **Load an existing termbase definition file**(as shown in the following screenshot), browse to the folder containing your glossary, and select the file with the name of your glossary (ending in .xdt). The **Open** dialog will display only .xdt files, so unless you have converted other glossaries in the same folder, you will see only the .xdt file that you are looking for.

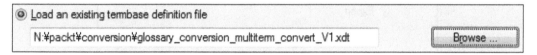

Follow the wizard through to completion (there should be no need to modify the settings), although you may wish to check in the **Descriptive Fields** screen to make sure that any picklist entries have been successfully added to fields of that type (such as the **Gender** field in our example).

Stage 3 – importing the content

At the end of Stage 2, you will have a newly created, empty termbase open in MultiTerm. Alternatively, if you are importing your glossary into a preexisting termbase, you will, at this point, open that termbase in MultiTerm via **File | New | Create Termbase**. In this final stage of the conversion process, we will import into the termbase the terms themselves, which are stored in the .mtf.xml file created by MultiTerm Convert in Stage 1, as follows:

1. In MultiTerm, click the **Termbase Management** button. In the **Catalog Categories** pane, under the name of the termbase, choose **Import**, then right-click and choose **Process**, as shown in the following screenshot:

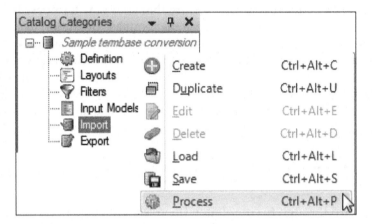

2. When the wizard starts, in the first screen (**General Settings**), under **Import file**, click **Browse** and navigate to the folder that contains your glossary (it normally appears automatically). Select the file with the name of your glossary (ending in .mtf.xml). Select the **Fast import** option. We know that the import file is compliant with MultiTerm XML because it was created in MultiTerm Convert. If this option is not selected, you will be asked in the next screen to create an exclusion file that will list any import errors. The results of doing this for the file in our example are as shown in the following screenshot:

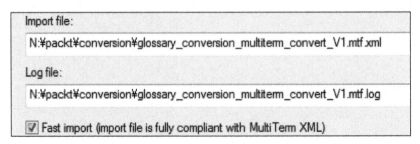

3. Click **Next**. You will see a screen telling you the number of entries processed. Click **Next** again, and then **Finish**.

4. To see your newly imported termbase entries in MultiTerm, click the **Terms** button and then the **Browse** tab just above it, as shown in the following screenshot:

Importing into an existing termbase

If you are going to import term lists into a preexisting termbase, ensure that any columns in your Excel glossary that correspond to existing fields in your termbase have exactly the same header as those fields.

Language column headers in the glossary must be exactly the same as those of the corresponding fields in MultiTerm; for example, French should be named French and not Fre, otherwise you may not be able to import your content (.mtf.xml) file into MultiTerm in Stage 3 of the process described in the preceding steps.

Columns in the Excel glossary corresponding to descriptive fields in the termbase should have exactly the same name as those in the termbase, or they will be imported as a new, additional field in Stage 3.

Imported terms with an already existing entry in the termbase are added as duplicate entries. It is therefore a good idea, if practicable, to remove duplicate rows from the Excel glossary before conversion. Alternatively, you can delete any duplicated entries in MultiTerm after import.

 If you are going to convert glossaries regularly, best practice is therefore to create a template Excel glossary that meets all of your needs and use that same format for all of your glossaries. You can then be assured that they will convert successfully.

Summary

In this chapter, you learned how to create a termbase in MultiTerm and interact with it in Trados Studio, and how to import existing glossaries for use during translation.

Working with Files from Earlier Versions of Trados

In this appendix, we show you how to convert TMs in .tmw (SDL Trados 2007) and other formats, and use bilingual Translator's Workbench and TagEditor files in SDL Trados Studio.

Converting SDL Trados 2007 memories

In this section, we describe how to convert TMs in SDL Trados 2007 and other formats for use in SDL Trados Studio. SDL refers to this process as upgrading a TM. You can upgrade TMs with different language pairs and file formats in one operation. Supported TM file types are .tmw (SDL Trados 2007), .mdb (SDLX), .tmx (exported from any .tmx compatible TM program), .txt (SDL Workbench and Winalign export), and .sdltm (SDL Trados Studio, primarily so that you can merge .sdltm TMs with TMs in other formats during the upgrade process).

To convert TMs in SDL Trados 2007 and other formats for use in SDL Trados Studio, perform the following steps:

1. In the **Welcome** or **Translation Memories** view, click the **Upgrade Translation Memories** button, shown in the following screenshot:

2. In the **Input Translation Memories** screen, to add the TMs that you want to convert to the current .sdltm format, choose one of the options shown at the top of the following screenshot. Once added, the TMs are listed with the number of TUs (translation units) in each TM shown on the right.

Add File-based TMs from Folder...	Add File-based TMs...	Add Server-based TM ▾	Remove	
Name	Location			Translation Units
english-german-united-nations.tmw	N:\packt\Learning Trados Studio\upgrade\T7 only\english-german-united-nation...			2837
english-german-eu.tmw	N:\packt\Learning Trados Studio\upgrade\T7 only\english-german-eu.tmw			2837

3. In the first **Output Translation Memories** screen, choose whether to produce a separate SDL Trados Studio **output memory** for each input memory (**Create output translation memory for each input translation memory**), group input memories with the same language pair into a single **output memory** (**Create output translation memory for each language pair**), or a combination of both these options (**Custom**).

4. In the next **Output Translation Memories** screen, you will specify various options for the output memories, doing so separately for each one. First select the name of the output memory on the left, as shown in the following screenshot:

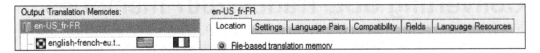

Output Translation Memories:	en-US_fr-FR					
en-US_fr-FR	Location	Settings	Language Pairs	Compatibility	Fields	Language Resources
english-french-eu.t...	◉ File-based translation memory					

Now configure the options under each tab separately for each TM, as follows:

1. In the **Location** tab, specify the folder where you want the output memories to go.

2. In the **Settings** tab, the options are as follows:

    ○   **Enable character-based concordance search**: Runs concordance searches based on groups of characters as well as words, to produce more fuzzy matches. This setting can be useful in highly inflected languages (such as Slavic languages), but can slow down concordance searches in large translation memories.

    ○   **Settings**: Choose whether to recognize text in various categories (dates, times, numbers, acronyms, variables, and measurements) as placeables in the output memory. For further details, see the SDL help files at http://tinyurl.com/trados-recognition-settings.

○ **Import translation units as plain text**: This option strips out tags and internal formatting in the input memories (useful if tags and formatting are likely to reduce the match levels from the output memories, particularly if you upgrade SDL Trados 2007 or other TMs populated while working directly in MS Word).

3. In the **Compatibility** tab, you can try to improve the degree of matching that the TM will produce by deciding how the storage data in the input memories gets imported. For details, see the SDL help files at `http://tinyurl.com/trados-compatibility`. These options constitute fine-tuning, so for most purposes, you can safely leave the default option selected.

4. In the **Fields** tab, you can optionally remove or rename existing fields in the input memories (for more information on TM fields, see *Appendix B, Managing Translation Memories*).

5. In the **Language Resources** tab, Language Resources is the collective name for TM settings that affect segmentation, such as custom abbreviations and variable lists. Choose to accept the default segmentation options in SDL Trados Studio (**Default Language Resources**) or (if available) click the drop-down arrow on the right to upgrade any existing settings in the import memories (**Upgraded Language Resources**).

6. Click **Finish** to run the upgrade process. For information on the number of TUs upgraded, click the **Details** link, shown on the right of the following screenshot. To open the upgraded TM in the **Translation Memories** view, click the **Open** link by the name of each TM.

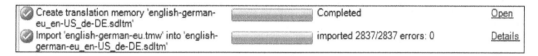

7. Click **Close**. When prompted to delete the temporary files, click **Yes**.

Importing TTX and ITD files

You can import `.ttx` (TagEditor) and `.itd` (SDLX) files directly into an `.sdltm` TM. The advantage of this approach is that SDL Trados Studio can generate **context matches** by taking into account the segment sequence in the `.ttx` or `.itd` files. However, unlike in the **Upgrade Translation Memories** approach described in the preceding section, it is not possible to import **TM fields** or **Language Resources**, because `.ttx` or `.itd` files do not store this information.

In the following example, we import some `.ttx` files:

1. In the **Translation Memories** view, click **Open** (*Alt + Shift + O*) to open the SDL Trados Studio TM that you want to import into. In the Navigation pane at the top-left, right-click the TM and choose **Import**.

2. In the **Import Files** screen, choose **Add Files** and browse to select the `.ttx` (or `.itd`) files.

3. The **Bilingual Document Import Options** screen lists various confirmation levels available in SDL Trados Studio. Leave the default options selected.

4. In the **General Import Options** screen, click **Finish**. The options in this screen are discussed in *Appendix B, Managing Translation Memories*.

Opening TTX and ITD files in the Editor

Bilingual files in `.ttx` and `.itd` format can be opened directly for translation or editing in SDL Trados Studio via the **Translate Single Document** command. When you choose **File | Save Target As**, you are prompted to save the target file as `.ttx` or `.itd`, or in its original file format. Files in `.ttx` and `.itd` format can also be incorporated in a project as translatable project files, including in combination with files in other formats.

Opening bilingual Word files in the Editor

Bilingual Word documents produced in SDL Trados Translator's Workbench can be opened directly in SDL Trados Studio, or added to a project as translatable project files.

 If you are using Translator's Workbench to pre-translate files, in the **Translate** window, check the option **Segment unknown sentences**. This ensures that any segments without a match in your SDL Trados 2007 translation memory are present and segmented in the newly generated bilingual Word document.

Summary

In this appendix, you learned various ways to upgrade and use TMs and other files not created in SDL Trados Studio. In *Appendix B, Managing Translation Memories*, we look at various ways to manage the data inside your TMs, including the process of creating TM data from previously translated, source and target document pairs by aligning them into a TM.

B
Managing Translation Memories

In this appendix, we look at how to maintain and modify the data in translation memories. We show you how to import and export data in SDL Trados Studio TMs and filter, modify, or delete their content. These techniques are useful when, for example, you want to merge one TM with another, or modify a term used in different segment contexts in a TM. We also discuss TM fields, which provide a way to label, categorize, and identify data in TM segments. We then go on to discuss alignment, the process of populating TM segments from pairs of previously translated source and target documents.

Maintaining translation memories

In this section, we will discuss various ideas for maintaining the data in your TMs.

Opening a TM

To modify the content of a TM, you must first open it in the **Translation Memories** view. In the **Translation Memories** view, choose **Open Translation Memory**, navigate to the TM that you want to open, and open it. The TM opens in a list at the top of the Navigation pane, as shown in the following screenshot:

To view information such as the file location, creation date and number of translation units (TUs) in the TM, right-click the name of the TM and choose **Settings**. The central pane of the **Translation Memories** view displays the first segments of the TM that you have opened (and any others that you have opened already will be visible via their tabs).

Finding and replacing text in a TM

You can search and/or replace text in the **Translation Memories** view using a technique similar to that used on text in bilingual SDLXLIFF files.

Standard find and replace operations

To bring up the standard **Find** or **Find and Replace** window, in the **Home** tab, click the **Find** (*Ctrl* + *F*) or **Replace** (*Ctrl* + *H*) button.

The **Find and Replace** window is shown in the following screenshot. Notice that you can replace text in the source as well as in the target in the TUs inside the TM.

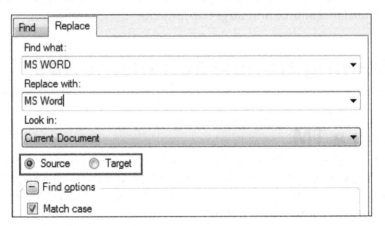

When you have run the replace operation, the background color of any TU whose content has been replaced changes to indicate that the TU has been edited, as shown in the following screenshot:

The changes you make are pending until you confirm them with **Commit Changes**, or discard them with **Discard TU Changes**, shown in the following screenshot:

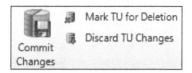

If the **Discard TU Changes** button is grayed out, you may be able to access it by right-clicking on the TU in the side-by-side pane instead. Once confirmed, these changes cannot be reversed, so it is wise to make a backup copy of your TM before you make such changes to your TM.

Finding text in both source and target

The search window at the top of the **Translation Memories** view allows you to run more complex searches as well as the basic find and replace operations described in the preceding section using the standard **Find and Replace** function. To run a basic search for TUs containing certain text strings, in the **Search Details** pane, shown in the following screenshot, type the search string in either or both of the **Source Text** or **Target Text** fields and press *Enter* or click **Perform Search**. Segments containing the search string are displayed in the side-by-side view.

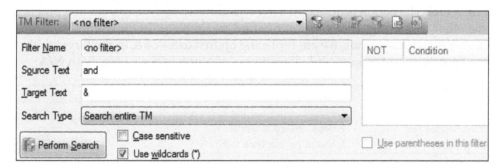

By searching for text in both source and target, you can find TUs that simultaneously match different conditions in both. In our example, we search for and in the source and & in the target to find TUs in which and has been translated as &. This example finds TUs like that shown in the following screenshot:

Only the number of TUs set in **File | Options | Translation Memories View | Number of translation units per page** are displayed in each page. To move from page to page, use the buttons in the **Home** view, shown in the following screenshot:

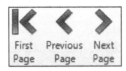

To redisplay all of the TUs, clear the **Source Text** or **Target Text** fields and click **Perform Search** again.

Running multiple find and replace operations

The search window at the top of the **Translation Memories** view also allows you to run several find and replace operations at once. To do this, from the **Home** tab, in the **Tasks** group, click the **Batch Edit** toolbar button shown in the following screenshot:

In the **Batch Edit** dialog box, click **Add** and choose **Find and Replace Text**. Type the text strings, specify whether to search in the source or target and match the case, and click **OK**. The action is added to a list of actions to be run. Repeat this process for the other text strings that you want to find and replace. In the example shown in the following screenshot, we are replacing all instances of **&** in the target with **et** (the French word for and), and all instances of **None** in the source with **N/A**:

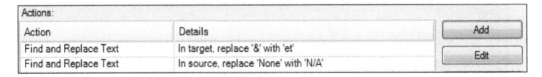

To run the find and replace operation on all of the actions that you have added to the list in this way, click **Finish** and then **Close**.

The search window at the top of the **Translation Memories** view makes the changes to the affected TUs as soon as you click **Finish**. You are not asked to confirm the changes, and once you replace text in the TM in this way, the changes cannot be undone. It is therefore wise to make a backup copy of your TM before you proceed.

Filtering text to find and replace

Filters are used to isolate TUs with certain characteristics so that you can edit, delete, or view them together in a single operation. For example, you could specify TUs that were added by a certain user, before a certain date, or that contain a particular piece of text, or that match all of these conditions. Filters can also be used to import and export matching data from TMs.

The **System Fields** pane on the right of the side-by-side view shows various information about the selected TU, such as when and by whom it was created and last modified, as shown in the following screenshot:

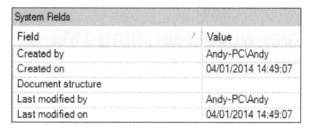

System Fields	
Field	Value
Created by	Andy-PC\Andy
Created on	04/01/2014 14:49:07
Document structure	
Last modified by	Andy-PC\Andy
Last modified on	04/01/2014 14:49:07

The following example assumes that we want to specify all TUs modified after a certain date.

To create the filter, in the **Search Details** pane, click the **Add Filter** icon, shown on the left of the following screenshot along with the **Save Filter** and **Delete Filter** icons:

Under **Filter Name**, type a name for the filter. On the lower right-hand side of the **Search Details** pane, click the **Add** button to open the **Add Condition** dialog box and set the options shown in the following screenshot:

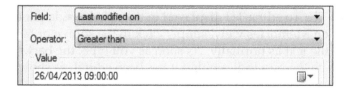

Field:	Last modified on
Operator:	Greater than
Value	
26/04/2013 09:00:00	

To create filters with multiple conditions, click **Add** to add a further condition. In the **AND/OR** column, choose **AND** to specify that both conditions must be satisfied, or choose **OR** to specify that either condition will suffice.

With dates, the operators **Smaller than** and **Greater than** signify earlier than and later than. With text content fields such as **Source segment**, the operators **Equal to** and **Contains** mean that the TU includes either *only* the specified text and *at least* the specified text, respectively.

Click the **Save Filter** button. The following screenshot shows the configured filter:

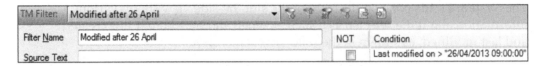

Applying filters when searching TMs

To find text with a filter, in the **Search Details** window, in the **TM Filter** list, select the filter, type any text that you want to search for, and click **Perform Search**. To search for all TUs that match the filter criteria, leave the **Source Text** and **Target Text** fields blank. In the case of the filter shown in the preceding screenshot, this approach could be used to find TUs that contain certain text strings and were modified after a certain date.

To apply filters to batch edit operations, described earlier in this chapter, click the **Batch Edit** toolbar button. Under **Filter**, select the filter, then search and replace as described earlier in this appendix.

Editing and deleting TUs

You can modify the content of the TUs displayed in the side-by-side pane of the **Translation Memories** view by using the find and replace methods described earlier in this appendix. Alternatively, you can click inside individual TUs and edit them directly.

To edit TUs directly, the following actions are available:

- **To edit a TU**: To edit a TU displayed in the side-by-side pane of the **Translation Memories** view, simply click in the source or target and add or delete the text as normally. As soon as you type, the background color of the TU changes to indicate that it has been edited, as shown in the following screenshot:

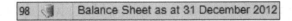

  The changes you make are pending until you confirm them with **Commit Changes**, or discard them with **Discard TU Changes**, as described earlier in this appendix in the section titled *Finding and replacing text in a TM*.

- **To delete a TU**: To delete a TU, you must first mark it for deletion with **Mark TU for Deletion** (shown in the screenshot in the earlier section titled *Standard find and replace operations*) and then confirm the deletion. Deleted TUs cannot be restored.

    ° To mark a TU for deletion, right-click in the TU and choose **Mark TU for Deletion** (*Ctrl + D*). The background color of the TU changes as shown in the following screenshot:

    ° To delete any TUs marked for deletion, choose **Commit Changes**. To discard the changes, choose **Discard TU Changes**.

- **To delete all TUs matching certain conditions**: Click the **Batch Delete** button (shown in the following screenshot) to open the **Batch Delete** window, select the relevant filter, and click **Finish**:

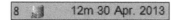

 If you click **Finish** in the **Batch Delete** window with no filter selected, you will delete the entire content of the TM. The **Batch Delete** feature can be dangerous in this sense, so make a backup of your TM first and use this feature with caution.

Importing and exporting TMs

Importing and exporting TM data is useful in a number of situations. For example, you can merge data from one TM into another as a way to combine TMs with different sublanguages, such as U.S. and U.K. English, so that you can get matches from TUs that were originally created with a different sublanguage from the one in your TM. You can also exchange data with TM tools other than SDL Trados Studio, for example if you want to share TM data with another translator who does not have access to SDL Trados Studio.

To import and export TM data, the TM must be visible in the Navigation pane of the **Translation Memories** view. To open the TM in this way, click **Open Translation Memory** (*Alt + Shift + O*) and select the TM as described earlier in this appendix under the *Opening a TM* section.

Exporting a TM

SDL Trados Studio uses the .tmx format to export TMs. In the Navigation pane, right-click the name of the TM and choose **Export**, as shown in the following screenshot:

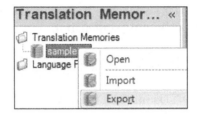

Under **Export to**, navigate to the location where you want the exported .tmx memory to go (if you do not do so, you may not be able to find your exported file later), and type a name for the exported TM. To export only TUs matching certain criteria, click **Edit** and add a filter as described earlier in this appendix. Click **Finish** to export the TUs.

Importing a TM

You can import data into a TM that is empty or already contains TUs, from .tmx or the bilingual file formats .sdlxliff, .ttx, or .itd (or a mixture of these formats). To import data into a TM, perform the following steps:

1. In the Navigation pane, right-click the name of the TM into which you want to import data and choose **Import**.

2. In the **Import Files** screen, choose **Add Files** and select the import file(s).

3. In the **TMX Import Options** and **Bilingual Document Import Options** screens (which of these screens appears depends on the import format), add a filter if desired. For information on the various .tmx import scenarios, see the SDL help files at http://tinyurl.com/trados-import-scenarios. Otherwise, leave the default options and click **Next**.

4. In the **General Import Options** screen, the most often used options are:

   ° **Import translation units as plain text**: This option removes any formatting tags from the imported TUs (useful if you think that the formatting and tags in the imported TUs will negatively affect the match levels from the TM later). This applies mostly to TMs created in tools working in MS Word.

    ◦   **Overwrite existing translation units**: If this option is selected, existing TUs in the TM with the same source but a different target segment to the imported TU are replaced with the target segment of the imported TU. If not, the TU is added to the TM as an alternative translation for the same source segment.

For more detail, see `http://tinyurl.com/trados-import-options`.

5. Click **Finish** to import the data.

Merging memories with different sublanguages

To import TUs with different sublanguages to that of the TM into which you are importing, under **General Import Options** in the **Import Wizard**, leave the **Exclude language variants** option *unselected*. To merge two TMs, for example, with the source languages French (France) and French (Canada) respectively, export one of the memories to `.tmx` and then import it into the other.

Working with TM fields

TM fields are labels that you can add to the TUs in the TM as you store each segment during translation, or by editing TUs in the **Translation Memories** view. For example, you could create a predefined **Subject** picklist with possible values **IT**, **Law**, and **EU**, or a text field in which you can type any desired text (such as by adding a job ID each time you start a new assignment). You can then assign one or more of these values to each TU as you translate. When using the TM subsequently, you can then create a filter to impose a penalty that will alert you to matches that do not correspond to one or more of these values. For example, if you have set up a field to identify whether a document concerns Microsoft or Apple products, you could use it to flag segments that come from Apple documents when translating a document about Microsoft. You can also use fields to filter the TUs during import and export operations.

Using TM fields during translation

To make use of TM fields during translation, perform the following steps:

• **To create a field**: Open the TM in the **Translation Memories** view. You cannot add new fields to the TM if it is open in the side-by-side pane, so close it by clicking the **Close Document (X)** icon on the right-hand side of the side-by-side pane. Now right-click on the name of the TM in the Navigation pane, and choose **Settings | Fields and Settings**.

Type a **Name** for the field, and choose the **Type**. If you are creating a list, click under **Picklist** and add the options to choose from, one by one. Select the **Allow Multiple Values** checkbox if you want to be able to assign more than one list value per TU. For example, if you were translating a contract relating to computers, the subject fields **IT** and **Law** would both apply. The following screenshot shows a completed field setting:

Name	Type	Picklist		Allow Multiple Values
Subject	List	IT,Law,EU	▾	☑

You can add fields and values at any time by returning to these settings.

- **To apply fields during translation**: Once you have created fields in your TM, you can use them to label the TUs that you add to the TM as you translate. For example, if you use the same TM for work from different clients, you could add a "Client" field so that each TU in the TM would carry an indication of which client it applies to.

  With a document open in the **Editor** view, choose **Project | Project Settings | Language Pairs | All Language Pairs | Translation Memory and Automated Translation**, then choose **Update** and select the previously added **Field Values** to apply to the TUs in the TM with which you are working. Field values in matched TUs appear on the right of the **Translation Memory Results** window, as in the following screenshot:

- **Updating existing TUs**: If the field allows multiple values, values not already assigned to the TU are added to those already assigned. If the field does not allow multiple values, values already assigned are replaced. To add the segment to the TM as an alternative translation with different field values, press *Ctrl + Shift + U*.

Filtering on TM fields during translation

In this example, we add a filter using the **Subject** field from the preceding section to impose a 1% penalty on matches from the TM that do not have the **Subject** value EU. This may be because we are doing a translation for the EU and want to be alerted if the TM gives us matches that do not have that subject, in case the proposed translation is unsuitable for an EU text.

To add a filter to a TM in use for a translation, in the **Editor** view, choose **Project Settings**. Under **Translation Memory and Automated Translation**, choose **Filters**, and then click **Add** and type a name for the filter. Click **Add** again. In the **Add Condition** dialog box, choose **Subject** and **Contains**, and select **EU** in the **Value** list. This situation is shown in the following screenshot:

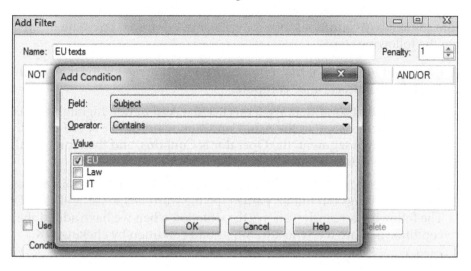

Click **OK** twice to exit.

As you translate in the **Editor**, if there is a match whose **Subject** value does not include **EU**, the **Translation Memory Results** window shows that the filter penalty has been applied, as in the following screenshot:

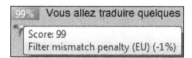

Using a filter to modify fields in the TM

You may sometimes need to modify the fields that are assigned to TUs in an existing TM. For example, you may want to add field values to TUs that have not yet been assigned any values, or to change the value assigned to TUs containing certain terms. When you add, replace, or remove fields and values in a TM, you will often want to apply the changes to certain TUs only rather than the entire TM. In this case, you must first create a filter to specify which TUs you want to update, otherwise all of the TUs in the TM will be affected.

In this example, we want to ensure that all TUs in the TM that contain both the source words **contract** and **computer** are updated to have the **Subject** labels **IT** and **Law**. We have created a picklist field **Subject** that allows multiple values to be selected from **IT**, **Law**, and **EU**. We will now create a filter (see the earlier section *Filtering text to find and replace*) to allow us to specify that only segments containing both the source words **contract** and **computer** will be updated. The filter will therefore contain two conditions, one for each of these words. To create this filter, perform the following steps:

1. Click **Add Filter** and under **Filter Name** type a name for the filter, such as **Contains "contract" and "computer"**.

2. To add the first condition, we then click the **Add** button highlighted in the following screenshot. In the **Add Condition** window, we specify that the **Field** is **Source segment**, the **Operator** is **Contains**, and then under **Value** we type the word contract, and click **OK**.

3. To add the second condition, we then click the **Add** button again and select the same settings but under **Value** type the word computer and click **OK**. The following screenshot shows the situation when we have added the first condition and are ready to add the second condition by clicking **OK**.

4. Click **Save Filter**.

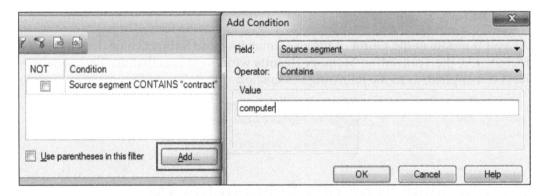

This results in a filter with two conditions, as shown in the following screenshot:

NOT	Condition	AND/OR
☐	Source segment CONTAINS "contract"	AND
☐	Source segment CONTAINS "computer"	

In the **Translation Memories** view, with the relevant TM open in the side-by-side pane, click the **Batch Edit** toolbar button. Under **Filter**, select the relevant filter. Click **Add** | **Change Field Value**. In the **Edit Action** dialog box, select the following settings:

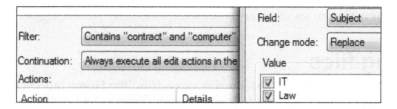

In the **Change mode** list, you can choose **Replace** to replace field values in TUs matching the filter with the selected values, **Add** to add the selected values to the existing ones, or **Remove** to remove the selected values. In this example, we are going to use the Replace action to ensure that the field values for any matching TUs get updated with the new values. Click **OK** and then **Finish** to update the fields. A window appears indicating how many TUs have been edited.

In our example, the **Subject** value for all TUs containing the source words **contract** and **computer** is now replaced with two values, **IT** and **Law**.

Alignment

Alignment is the process of adding material to a TM from existing pairs of documents (source and translation) that were translated without using a TM tool. By aligning these files, you can recycle their content into a TM to use when you subsequently translate similar material in SDL Trados Studio or another TM tool.

Alignment can be time consuming, especially with large files in which the source and target documents have different segmentation (for example, if sentences in the source document have been split up into smaller sentences in the target document). In these situations, it is often worth spending time to prepare the documents themselves to ensure that their structures are similar before you align them. For example, identical structures created by keeping whole sentences together will improve alignment results.

The new alignment tool in SDL Trados Studio 2014 is particularly useful if you want to do a quick and dirty alignment in the knowledge that you are unlikely to re-use all of the aligned TUs anyway. It is therefore a good idea to import the alignment results into a separate TM used for reference purposes only in order to not contaminate your main TM(s) with incorrect alignments.

In SDL Trados Studio 2014, files are aligned into a SDL Trados Studio TM (`.sdltm`). Unlike with **WinAlign**, the alignment tool in previous versions, there is at the time of writing no dedicated post-alignment editor for correcting misaligned segments. Once you have aligned the segments, however, you can modify them by dragging and dropping text from one TU to another, spot-edit the source and target cells in the **Translation Memories** view, and remove erroneously paired segments.

Aligning files

In the **Welcome** or **Translation Memories** view, from the **Home** tab, click the **Align Documents** button, shown in the following screenshot:

To align your source and target files, perform the following steps:

1. In the **Select Translation Memory** window, shown in the following screenshot, choose to add an existing TM or create a new one, as described in *Chapter 2, Creating and Using Translation Memories*. You can import the aligned segments into an existing TM that already contains translation pairs or create a new, empty TM to import into.

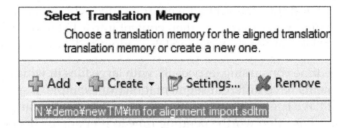

2. To add TM fields to the TM that you have added or created, you can optionally choose **Settings** | **Fields and Settings** at this point. To illustrate the usefulness of this, in our example, we will take the optional step of creating a text field called **Origin**, as shown in the following screenshot, which will allow us to later identify all of the segments that have been added to the TM by the alignment.

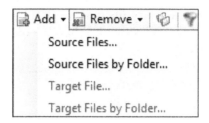

Fields				
Name	Type	Picklist	Allow Multiple Values	Add
Origin	Text		☐	

3. Back in the **Align Documents** wizard, click **Next**.

4. In the **Documents for Alignment** screen, part of which is shown in the following screenshot, click **Add** to add the source and target files. Files can be added individually or by selecting a folder. If you select a folder, all of the files in the folder and any subfolders it contains will be added. You must add the source files first and then the target files.

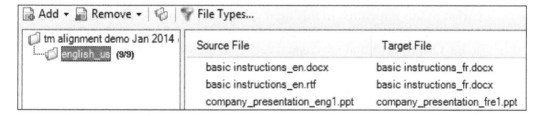

If you have added the files by folder rather than individually, you may need to click the relevant folder name on the left to display the files in the **Source File** and **Target File** panes on the right, as shown in the following screenshot:

Add ▾ Remove ▾ File Types...		
tm alignment demo Jan 2014	Source File	Target File
└ english_us (9/9)	basic instructions_en.docx	basic instructions_fr.docx
	basic instructions_en.rtf	basic instructions_fr.docx
	company_presentation_eng1.ppt	company_presentation_fre1.ppt

Click **Add** again and add the target files in the same way. If you add files by folder, files with matching filenames, including those in subfolders, will be paired up automatically. In our example, the digits **9/9** after the name of the source files folder on the left of the screenshot tell us that all nine source files have been paired with a target file.

To remove an incorrect target file and add the correct one, or to add a target file for a source file for which no partner was found automatically, in the **Target file** list, select the file and from the right-click menu, choose **Add target file** or **Remove target file**, as shown in the following screenshot:

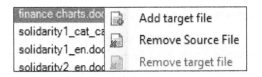

To remove incorrectly added files, select the file(s) and choose **Remove** and the appropriate option from the list. In the following screenshot, we manually remove a temporary file that was left in the source folder and mistakenly picked up for alignment. When the filenames are paired up correctly, click **Next**.

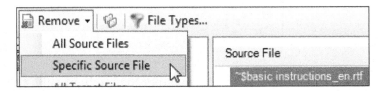

5. The **Alignment and TM Import Options** screen, shown in the following screenshot, offers the same options as when importing a TM described earlier in this appendix. In this example, under **Apply Field Values**, we have clicked **Edit** on the right and added a value (**Alignment Jan 7, 2014**) to the **Origin** field that we created earlier to identify the origin of the aligned segments.

The **Alignment quality value** is derived from a mechanism used by SDL Trados Studio to determine the reliability of the segment pairings (that is, the assumed probability that the pairing will be correct). For example, the default setting of 70% means that any segments given a reliability factor of less than 70% will not be aligned. It is worth experimenting with various values to obtain the best results. For more details on the logic behind this, see the SDL help pages at http://tinyurl.com/align-quality.

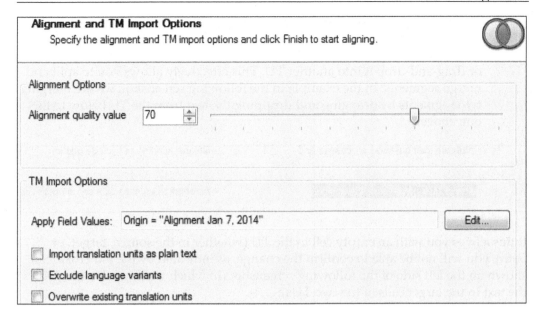

6. Click **Finish**. The **Aligning Documents** window lists the number of segments aligned for each source document, as shown in the following screenshot:

7. Click **Close**. The **Translation Memories** view now opens with the imported segments visible (if no segments are showing, press *F5* to refresh the view). The column on the right of the side-by-side view shows the **Origin** field that we created, along with default fields showing the source and target documents from which the aligned segment was generated. The **Field Values** pane on the right shows further meta-information for aligned segments, including the alignment **Quality** value (which in our example indicates a high reliability level of 93%).

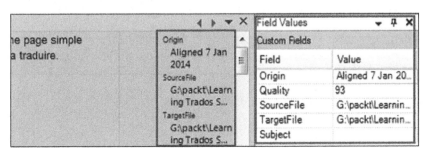

8. To check the results of the alignment, you can now review, spot-edit, and delete segments in the **Translation Memories** view, as described earlier in this appendix. You can also select text in one TU and either copy and paste or drag-and-drop it into another TU. This effectively allows you to split and merge segments. In the example in the following screenshot, we are merging two segments by dragging and dropping the text from the TU below to the one above:

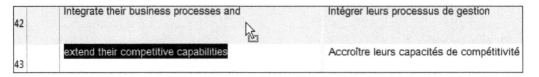

If this leaves you with an empty cell in the TU (whether in the source, target, or both), you will not be able to confirm the change, as indicated by the red cross icon shown on the left side of the following screenshot (in which we have also merged the text in the target cells of the two TUs):

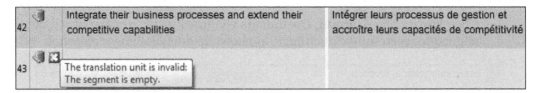

Assuming that you are happy to delete the TU from the TM, you can get round this problem by marking the TU with the empty cell(s) for deletion, via **Mark TU for Deletion**, as described earlier in this appendix. It will then be deleted when you confirm the other changes that you have made during this editing process (via **Commit Changes**). Alternatively, you can cancel the pending changes via **Discard TU Changes**.

To help you check segments of lower quality, you can create a filter on the **Quality** field to display only those segments in the side-by-side view, as shown in the following screenshot. In this example, we have set the field **Quality** to be **Smaller than or equal to** a value of **90**.

Filter Name	Alignment quality below 90		NOT	Condition
Source Text			☐	Quality <= "90"

Alignment penalty

When you translate a document in the **Editor** using the aligned TM, an alignment penalty of 1% is applied to any matches produced by alignment, as shown in the following screenshot. This is to alert you to the need to double-check matches from segments produced by alignment, which will in many cases of course be less reliable than those that you have added to a TM by translating a text in the **Editor**. Note that this can result in high levels of 99% matches in the **Analyze Files** report. To adjust the alignment penalty, under **Project Settings**, choose **Translation Memory and Automated Translation | Penalties**.

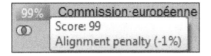

Summary

In this appendix, you learned how to manage data in your TMs, work with TM fields, and align previously translated documents into a new or existing TM.

Index

User Interface Language 14

V

Verification Message Details dialog box 90

W

Window
auto-hiding 52
closing 52
resizing 52
word counts
about 63
match types, categorizing 63, 64
Word documents
SDLXLIFFs, converting to 94, 95

About Packt Publishing

Packt, pronounced 'packed', published its first book "*Mastering phpMyAdmin for Effective MySQL Management*" in April 2004 and subsequently continued to specialize in publishing highly focused books on specific technologies and solutions.

Our books and publications share the experiences of your fellow IT professionals in adapting and customizing today's systems, applications, and frameworks. Our solution based books give you the knowledge and power to customize the software and technologies you're using to get the job done. Packt books are more specific and less general than the IT books you have seen in the past. Our unique business model allows us to bring you more focused information, giving you more of what you need to know, and less of what you don't.

Packt is a modern, yet unique publishing company, which focuses on producing quality, cutting-edge books for communities of developers, administrators, and newbies alike. For more information, please visit our website: www.packtpub.com.

Writing for Packt

We welcome all inquiries from people who are interested in authoring. Book proposals should be sent to author@packtpub.com. If your book idea is still at an early stage and you would like to discuss it first before writing a formal book proposal, contact us; one of our commissioning editors will get in touch with you.

We're not just looking for published authors; if you have strong technical skills but no writing experience, our experienced editors can help you develop a writing career, or simply get some additional reward for your expertise.

Oracle JRockit

The Definitive Guide

Develop and manage robust Java applications with Oracle's high-performance Java Virtual Machine

Foreword by Adam Messinger,
Vice President of Development in the Oracle Fusion Middleware group

Marcus Hirt   Marcus Lagergren   [PACKT] enterprise

Oracle JRockit:
The Definitive Guide

ISBN: 978-1-84719-806-8   Paperback: 588 pages

Develop and manage robust Java applications with Oracle's high-performance Java Virtual Machine

1. Learn about the fundamental building blocks of a JVM, such as code generation and memory management, and utilize this knowledge to develop code you can count on.

2. Realize the full potential of Java applications by learning how to apply advanced tuning and analysis.

3. Work with the JRockit Mission Control 3.1/4.0 tools suite to debug or profile your Java applications.

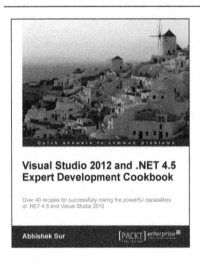

**Visual Studio 2012 and .NET 4.5
Expert Development Cookbook**

Over 40 recipes for successfully mixing the powerful capabilities
of .NET 4.5 and Visual Studio 2012

Abhishek Sur   [PACKT] enterprise

Visual Studio 2012 and .NET 4.5
Expert Development Cookbook

ISBN: 978-1-84968-670-9   Paperback: 380 pages

Over 40 recipes for successfully mixing the powerful capabilities of .NET 4.5 and Visual Studio 2012

1. Step-by-step instructions to learn the power of .NET development with Visual Studio 2012.

2. Filled with examples that clearly illustrate how to integrate with the technologies and frameworks of your choice.

3. Each sample demonstrates key concepts to build your knowledge of the architecture in a practical and incremental way.

Please check **www.PacktPub.com** for information on our titles

Corona SDK Application Design

ISBN: 978-1-84969-736-1   Paperback: 98 pages

A quick and easy guide to creating your very own mobile apps with Corona SDK

1. Build apps that can be used on multiple platforms.

2. Test your apps and publish them on GooglePlay and Apple's App store.

3. Develop your own apps with the help of interactive examples.

SignalR: Real-time Application Development

ISBN: 978-1-78216-424-1   Paperback: 124 pages

Utilize real-time functionality in your .NET applications with ease

1. Develop real-time applications across numerous platforms.

2. Create scalable applications that are ready for cloud deployment.

3. Utilize the full potential of SignalR.

Please check **www.PacktPub.com** for information on our titles

Lightning Source UK Ltd.
Milton Keynes UK
UKOW05f0818051217
313901UK00005B/469/P